# READING
## THE
# MUSLIM MIND

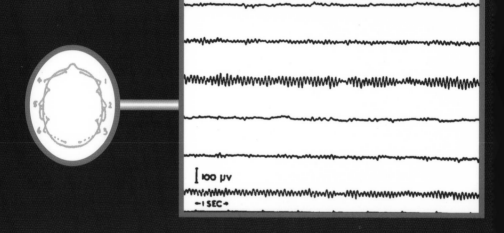

# HASSAN HATHOUT

## Foreword by Ahmad Zaki Yamani

# Reading The Muslim Mind

# READING
# THE MUSLIM MIND

# Hassan Hathout

*WITH A FOREWORD BY*
## Ahmad Zaki Yamani

American Trust Publications

American Trust Publications
2622 East Main Street
Plainfield, Indiana 46168–2703

Copyright © March 1995 American Trust Publications
All rights reserved
Printed in the United States of America

*Library of Congress cataloging in publication data*
Hathout, Hassan.
    Reading the Muslim Mind / Hassan Hathout; with a foreword
by Ahmad Zaki Yamani.
        p.    cm.
    Includes bibliographical references and index.
    ISBN 0-89259-156-0. — ISBN 0-89259-157-9 (pbk.)
    1. Islam.    I. Title.
BP161.2.H84    1994
297—dc20                                            94-46150
                                                      CIP

*TO THOSE WHO ARE COMMITTED*
*TO LOVE, TRUTH AND THE*
*HUMAN FAMILY*

# Acknowledgments

I thank God for enabling me to write this book, at long last, even though in my confinement during a period of illness, without which I would have probably kept procrastinating to a future that may have never come, under the illusion of "too busy." As the Quran says: *"It may be that you dislike a thing, and God brings about through it a great deal of good"* (4:19).

Prophet Muhammad said, "He who is thankless to people, is thankless to God." I therefore gratefully acknowledge the tremendous support, help and backing of my wife, Salonas, which by no means took me by surprise. It has been the pattern since we married forty-three years ago.

My thanks are also due to my brothers and friends who have continually prodded me to write, rightly maintaining that a written work is more durable than prolific speeches, necessary as they are.

I am particularly grateful to Mrs. Carol De Mars, a dear friend and a noble soul, for volunteering to diligently review the text and offering invaluable editorial advice.

To my publisher, I will always be indebted for making my task both easy and pleasurable.

Last but not least, my associate Miss Hedab Al-Tarifi bore the burden of prompt typing of the manuscript, never wearying of requests for alterations and readjustments. May God reward all of them.


*Hassan Hathout*

# Contents

# Foreword

Sheikh Ahmad Zaki Yamani*

Of all the major religions of the world, Islam stands apart in that it does not derive its name from a tribe or a person, like Judaism (from Judea), or Christianity (from Christ), or Buddhism (from Buddha). Islam does not derive its name from the prophet Muhammad, may God's peace and blessings be upon him, and in spite of the penchant of some past Orientalists for terms such as "Muhammadanism" and "Muhammadans," these are not names that Muslims accept for their faith or for themselves.

*Islam* derives from two sources, *taslim,* i.e. submission, and *salam,* i.e. peace, and it is, in essence, a complete and integrated ideology that governs the relation-

---

* Sheikh Ahmad Zaki Yamani is former Minister of Petrol and Mineral Resources, of the Kingdom of Saudi Arabia, and one of the most accomplished statesmen of our times. He is also an Islamic scholar in his own right and annually participates in the course on Islamic Shari'ah at Harvard University Law School. His book *The Everlasting Shari'ah* (Saudi Publishing House, 1970) and his numerous writings and lectures have gone far in elucidating the facts about Islam. He is the founder and chairman of the reputable Center for Global Energy Studies, based in London, England. He is also founder and chairman of Alfurqan: The Islamic Heritage Foundation, active in preserving, recording and publishing old Islamic manuscripts.

ship between man and his Creator and the relationships of human beings amongst themselves.

The relationship of the human being to the Almighty is one of absolute submission by the creature to the will of his or her Creator. This is the essential and general meaning of the word *Islam*, and it is a meaning that is not confined to the faith that was revealed through the prophet Muhammad. As a matter of fact the Quran refers to a number of prophets (God's peace be upon them all) who appeared before our prophet Muhammad as Muslims. Thus the religion of Abraham, and in fact of all the prophets, the Quran tells us, was Islam:

> . . .*the creed of your forefather Abraham. It is He (God) Who has named you Muslims, both before and in this (book), that the Apostle may be a witness for you, and you may be witnesses for mankind.* (22:78)

On the other hand, the relationships of human beings amongst themselves are governed by the second source of the word *Islam*—peace—which of course entails tolerance and mercy. In a description of the Muslim, our Prophet tells us that "the Muslim is he from whose tongue and hands other Muslims are safe." The Prophet also often heaped praise upon tolerance and the tolerant, as in his statement, "God is merciful towards the tolerant, he who is tolerant in selling and tolerant in buying."

In war, the rules of engagement, to borrow a modern phrase from the military, dictate that the Muslim may engage the non-Muslim in combat only if he is threatened by the latter. And this was the basis on which the divine consent for Muslims to fight was given. In the words of the Quran:

> *Permission (to fight) is given to those against whom war is being wrongfully waged—and verily God has indeed the power to succor them.* (22:39)

The relationship between Muslims and non-Muslims in general, and the People of the Book in particular, is a multifaceted subject that merits much more of a discussion than can be allowed in an introduction of this nature. Suffice it to say at this point that tolerance and peace are the twin principles that underlie that relationship. That is what is ordained by the texts of the Quran and the Prophet's sayings. As for the incidents in history that contradict these principles, they are attributable to the Muslims concerned and not to Islam, just as manifestations of un-Christian behavior must be attributed to individual Christians and not to the teachings of Jesus Christ (God's peace be upon him).

Islam is further distinguished by the fact that the Muslim who must be at peace with others must be also at peace with himself. This is a necessary effect of the Muslim's total submission to the will of God. Islam is unique in the compatibility and harmony it creates between the spiritual and material aspects of life. The Muslim's conduct in material matters is controlled and channelled by the spiritual teachings of his or her faith, as those familiar with Islamic law concerning business transactions or personal conduct may well appreciate. Worship in Islam, on the other hand, is a blend of verbal supplication and physical movements, the purpose of which is to confirm and emphasize the spiritual essence. The Muslim's daily prayers, for example, comprise several bodily movements. Of these, the *ruku'* (the bowing position) depicts the Muslim's humility before the greatness of his or her Lord as he or she repeats the words prescribed for this position, *"Glorified is my Lord the Great."* Likewise, the *sujud,* or position of prostration in prayer, depicts the trifling existence of the human being before the infinite majesty of the divine, and in this humble position the servant repeats the prescribed words, *"Glorified is my Lord the Exalted."* These postures and movements signify a Muslim's willingness to serve his Lord and Creator, reposing his trust and faith in His mercy and grace. Bowing and prostrations are expressive of the Muslim's extreme humility, which is reserved for God alone and no one else. Muslims are taught by the Quran to say:

> *Thee alone do we worship, and unto Thee alone do we turn for aid.* (1:5)

As for their dealings with fellow human beings, their faith dictates that they be based on equality.

The history of mankind has witnessed a number of civilizations: the Chinese, the Pharaonic, the Greek, the Persian and the Roman. It has also witnessed the Islamic civilization. Each of the civilizations that preceded Islam became renowned for aspects that distinguished it from the others. Thus philosophy thrived in the Greek civilization whereas architecture was the strong point of the Romans. The Islamic civilization, on the other hand, is notable in that it saw the rise of all major fields of knowledge, such as medicine, astronomy, chemistry, mathematics and philosophy, as well as architecture. But the most important feature that distinguishes the Islamic civilization from its predecessors is that we know the precise point in history when it was born, i.e. the date of the revelation of the Islamic faith to the Prophet in the seventh century C.E. By contrast, other civilizations took centuries to evolve and therefore to appear in a recognizable form. They did not have a precise starting period or date of birth, if we may use the expression. Furthermore, whereas other civilizations arose out of the social environments in which they were born, the seventh century Arabs of Makkah were not capable of establishing a civilization of which the hallmark was knowledge, for they were generally ignorant and illiterate. It was the prophet Muhammad's call (God's peace and blessing be upon him) that shook them to their foundations and turned their social structure upside down. They were transformed by that call and that divine message, and set off in every direction of the then known world, changing the course of history as they went along.

True, not all of the tribal Arab customs that prevailed before Islam were abolished by the Quran and the Prophet's *sunnah*.[†] Some were endorsed, others were modified and integrated in the new legal and moral order, whilst of course those that were inconsistent with Islam were done away with. Some of those customs that were not directly covered by the Quran

---

[†] *Sunnah*: Lit. "a way, course, rule, mode, or conduct of life," and in Islamic literature it is used to signify the example or mode of life of Prophet Muhammad, which is the second main source of Islamic law. Ed.

or the sunnah were later dealt with by the jurists and scholars who took on the task of interpreting the original texts, and it was through their conclusions that traces of some of the old, undesirable Bedouin customs found their way into the *Shari'ah* (body of Islamic law). This part of the Shari'ah, as we shall see later on, is not immutable and must always lend itself to scrutiny by the qualified jurists of every age. That, however, is a long and involved subject which would require long discourses and explanations. Nevertheless, one or two examples from the field of family law would illustrate this point.

Polygamy and the right of men to divorce wives at will were widely accepted and exercised in pre-Islamic Arabia. A man was allowed as many wives as he pleased and could divorce them and change them without restriction. This state of affairs continued into the first half of the Prophet's life (God's peace and blessings be upon him). Islam put a ceiling on the number of wives that a man could have at any one time and made the right to take more than one wife conditional upon his being able to treat them with equal fairness. Furthermore, the right to take more than one wife with these restrictions as originally ordained was closely connected with situations in which men had orphan children in their care. The Quran, in the following terms, threatened those who appropriated for themselves the property that rightfully belonged to orphans :

> *Behold, those who sinfully devour the possessions of*
> *orphans but fill their bellies with fire (in the life to*
> *come) and will have to endure a blazing flame.* (4:10)

Those Muslims to whom the property of orphans had been entrusted were alarmed, and fearing that part of that property mingled with their own for investment purposes might inadvertently be denied to the orphans, they sought to return to the Prophet the orphans' property to save themselves from falling foul of the divine law. At that stage another Quranic verse was revealed:

> *And if you have reasons to fear that you might not act equitably towards orphans, then marry from among women such as are lawful to you, two or three or four; but if you have reason to fear that you might not be able to treat them with equal fairness, then (only) one.... (4:3)*

Regrettably the legal tolerance of polygamy that was afforded by the Quran was often exploited by Muslims with scant regard for the conditions under which it was supposed to be exercised. Rather than view it with the utmost caution and seriousness that are warranted by the circumstances in which it was allowed and the conditions under which it was ordained, the right to polygamy was taken by the males of some societies simply as license to indulge in multiple sexual relationships.

Many of the Arabs in particular, once they acquired wealth, made polygamy the rule rather than the exception, and although they did not exceed the limit of four wives at a time, they resorted to divorce whenever the desire for change arose. They used divorce to attain worldly pleasures although they knew that while it was lawful, it was, in the words of the

Prophet (God's peace and blessings be upon him), "the most abhorred of lawful things to God." Furthermore, the Quran is quite clear on how this distasteful legal sanction is to be effected. When the marital relationship becomes strained and deteriorates, resort should first be made to arbitration:

> *And if you have reason to fear that a breach might occur between them, appoint an arbiter from among his people and an arbiter from among her people; if they both want to set things aright, God may bring about their reconciliation....* (4:35)

In the event that arbitration fails, the husband may implement one act of divorce, the effect of which would be suspended for a period of three months and ten days, after which the divorce goes into final effect. During this period of suspension, the wife must remain in the marital home so that her spouse may have the opportunity to reconsider the divorce, the legal remedy that is yet so abhorrent in the eyes of God. This form of divorce may be effected twice between husband and wife. If it occurs for a third time, then it becomes effective immediately, and the two are separated forever unless and until the woman marries another man and gets divorced from him. In the words of the Quran:

> *A divorce may be (pronounced) twice, whereupon the marriage must either be resumed in fairness or dissolved in a goodly manner....* (2:229)

> *And if he divorces her (finally) she shall therefore not be lawful unto him unless she first takes another hus-*

*band; then if the latter divorces her, there shall be no
sin upon either of the two if they return to one another—provided that both of them think that they will be
able to keep within the limits set by God....* (2:230)

In spite of the clarity of the Quran in this matter, Muslim husbands have sometimes put into effect all three divorces with one utterance. Some Muslim jurists, anxious to retain the cooling off period that the Quran allows for spouses to reconsider, held that three divorces effected with one utterance or at the same time, count as only one divorce. However when Omar ibn Al-Khattab, the second caliph after the Prophet, saw how lightly people were treating the grave matter of divorce, he ruled that the pronouncement of three divorces would put into effect all three. Furthermore, the Prophet's teachings on the matter stipulate that a man may not divorce his wife in some specified circumstances, such as during her period of menstruation or during the time between two menstrual cycles if, in that time, sexual contact has occurred (coitus is prohibited during menstruation). When one of the Prophet's companions, Abdullah ibn Omar, was in breach of this rule, the Prophet ordered him to return to his wife.

These are examples of the regrettable practices in some Muslim societies that have led to the distorted view of our legal system held by some observers. In spite of this, however, the Shari'ah, especially those parts of it that concern women and constitutional matters, remains a unique legal system in what it affords to the protection of human rights and the organization of societies and individuals.

It is indeed unfortunate that these brilliant aspects of the Shari'ah, which serves humanity like no other legal system does, should be eclipsed by the tendency of some Muslims to exaggerate the harshness of the concept of punishment in Islam. This is the result of a serious misunderstanding of Islam to which Muslims, let alone alien orientalists, have fallen victim. Islam was not revealed in order to amputate the thieving hand or to stone the fornicator, but rather it came to protect and safeguard human dignity. The harshness of punishment for the offender is meant more as a deterrent than for prompt application. This is borne out by the fact that many obstacles have to be over-come before punishment can be effected—the burden of proof is so onerous that implementing the punish-ment can be practically impossible.

Small wonder then that the genuinely Islamic soci-ety is characterized by kindness and congeniality. These are some of the requirements prescribed by Islam for the establishment of a civilization of high order. And of course, the component units that make up this civilized society, human beings, must be of the highest caliber, molded by the ideals specified by their Creator.

However, the allure of worldly temptations has taken its toll on Muslims' adherence to their Lord's commands and it is unrealistic to expect to find in today's Muslim society many whose conduct and behav-ior is wholly Islamic. In my own life's experience, I have met only a handful, and I can categorically state that Dr. Hassan Hathout is one of them. I was therefore very pleased indeed at his request that I write the introduc-tion to his book *Reading the Muslim Mind*. Reading his thoughts, even before reading his book, have helped me embark on a voyage to a world of "realistic ideals."

Dr. Hathout understands Islam in its real sense, as it should be understood. His belief in God and in His oneness therefore is not only the result of his acceptance of the divine revelation and the Prophet's teachings, but it is as well a product of a vigorous mental exercise in which logic and reasoning are applied. Such mental effort is in compliance with numerous Quranic exhortations to man to think, ponder and deliberate the universe and his or her own existence within the universe, as this enhances the human being's knowledge of the Creator. To quote the Quran:

> *Surely in the creation of the heavens and the earth,*
> *and in the alternation of night and day, there are signs*
> *for men of understanding.* (3:190)

> *Those who remember Allah while standing, sitting or*
> *(reclining) on their backs, and reflect on the creation*
> *of the heavens and the earth (saying) "Our Lord! You*
> *have not created this in vain. Glory to You!"* (3:191)

Hence the book's first chapter, entitled "God," draws a path that can lead the Muslim to the knowledge of his Lord and therefore facilitate belief and total acceptance. His style is at once convincing to the young and persuasive to the mature non-believing adult. His logical analysis of the factors pointing to the existence of God lead him, in the second chapter, to a further logical analysis of the consequences of the existence of God, as manifested in the human being, in the resurrection and posthumous life, in the difference between man and beast, and in the three major monotheistic religions that had a common starting point in the person of the patriarch Abraham, namely Judaism, Christianity and Islam.

The third chapter of the book is an interesting and objective exposition of Islam and its relationship with the other two religions. The non-Muslim reader who has no knowledge of Islam will be astonished at the bonds that link Islam with Christianity in particular. The Quran tells us:

> . . .*And you will surely find that of all people, they who say: "We are Christians" are closest to feeling affection for those who believe. This is because there are priests and monks among them, and because they are not arrogant.* (5:82)

The Islamic civilization has left its clear imprint on the civilization of the West in various disciplines and in the arts. It gave the Western world the foundation on which it could build its own civilization, as is indicated by the liberal use of adapted forms of Arabic words or their translations.

The Arabic word for "university," *jami'ah*, for example, has its origins in the word *jami'*, which is the word for a larger mosque in a town or locality. It was in mosques that disciplines such as medicine, astronomy and law were first taught, with students seated in a circle around their teachers. This was emulated in the West in the sense that special buildings for teaching were established and were given the name that corresponds in meaning to the Arabic *jami'*, i.e. the Latin word, *universitas*, or *university* in modern English. The degree that the Muslim student was awarded for the successful completion of his studies was the *ijazah,* which corresponds in meaning to the word *license,* which is of course the name of the academic degree in some European countries.

It should be known by now that the past rift between Muslims and Christians had political roots. It was not caused by the advent of Islam as a religion, and as the author points out, it is wrong to describe the dominant civilization of today as Judeo-Christian. That is just an attempt to blot out the proven historical facts which show the considerable influence of the early Muslims on this civilization, much greater, in fact, than that of the Jews. Today's civilization therefore is more aptly described as Judeo-Christian-Islamic. This chapter reveals the extent of the esteem in which the Quran holds Moses, the prophet of the Jews. The story of the struggle of Moses and his people is repeated several times in the Quran, and in fact the name of Moses recurs many more times than that of our prophet Muhammad, God's peace and blessings be upon them both. The names of the prophets Ishmael, Isaac, Jacob, Moses, Aaron, David, Solomon and Joseph are popular in the Islamic community. All this indicates that the dispute between the Muslims and the Jews is political in nature and not religious. As a matter of fact, the Jews would probably be the first to admit that they enjoyed more security and better treatment in the Islamic state than anywhere else. When Islamic rule came to an end in Spain, the Jews there fled from the new rulers to another Islamic state, that of the Ottomans.

By the same token, the bonds of tolerance and cooperation between the Islamic and Christian worlds can be extremely strong, given the requisite sincerity and political will. The differences between the two religions do not call for enmity and there exist sufficient common interests that warrant putting an end to the trail of injustices that have been and continue to be inflicted on Muslims. It is time to put an end to all that and join hands in removing the bitterness and resentment that have built up over the ages.

The fourth chapter of the book, one of the longest and most important, analyzes the anatomy of Islam. Dr. Hathout briefly surveys the Shari'ah, or body of Islamic law, the separation of religion from state, and democracy. He goes on to deal with the spiritual aspect of Islam, i.e. matters of worship and the moral message that disciplined Muslims and implanted in them compassion, mercy and the love for everything good. I would just wish to add to Dr. Hathout's very interesting explanation of the Shari'ah another important point: A clear distinction must be made between two things: on the one hand, there are the Quranic rules and commands—very few in number—and the rules embodied in the proven utterances and deeds of the Prophet, all of which form a sacred and immutable source of law; on the other hand, there is the vast body of legal opinions produced by Muslim jurists and scholars from all sects over the ages. These latter laws are not religiously binding on Muslims and are therefore not considered sacred or immutable.

One of the sources of Islamic law is what the jurists call the *masalih mursalah*, which can be loosely translated as "the public interest." The early jurists used this source to lay down new rules to cover situations that did not exist in the Prophet's lifetime and therefore are not provided for in the texts, i.e. the Quran and sunnah. The jurists further used the principle of public interest as a guiding light in which the provisions of the texts could be interpreted. Some went even further, giving precedence to public interest over the texts where there was conflict between the two, a rather radical step that is difficult to imagine.

The search continues incessantly for solutions to the new problems that arise with the changing times and the accompanying changes in the needs of the Islamic community. Hence the need for the Shari'ah to develop. Its development started very shortly after the Prophet's death, and one of the most daring figures in bringing about changes was the second caliph, Omar ibn Al-Khattab, who went so far as to adapt or suspend some of the Quranic provisions.[‡] This introduction is not, of course, the right place for a full explanation of these matters, so I shall restrict my comments to drawing a distinction between the two major schools of thought on the matter of *ijtihad,* or juristic reasoning, one favoring a close adherence to the text and its literal interpretation without much thought to its objectives, the other looking more for purpose and wisdom underlying the legal enactments.

Dr. Hathout has narrated the story of the soldiers who were ordered not to perform the *asr* (mid-afternoon) prayer except in Bani Quraidha territory. When the time for the asr prayer approached its end without their having arrived at their destination, some of them chose to perform their prayer, on the basis of their

---

[‡] Caliph Omar's decision was, however, not arbitrary, but based on his understanding and interpretation of the Quranic injunctions and their application to the prevalent situation in the land. On all such occasions he consulted the learned companions of the Prophet who were present and formed his advisory council; they all agreed with him. Ed.

interpreting the Prophet's command not as meaning that they should refrain from praying, but that they should go with great dispatch to their target. The rest of the soldiers chose the literal interpretation of the Prophet's order and abstained from praying until they had reached their destination. Later, the Prophet (God's peace and blessing be upon him) approved both interpretations as being correct, since both had been based on a sound premise. Omar ibn Al-Khattab, in his ijtihad, belonged to the school that looked more to the wisdom and purpose of the enactments than to the literal meaning of the texts. My reading of Dr. Hathout's views on how to interpret the enactments or adapt or develop them to cover new and ever-changing situations indicates that he leans toward the same school.

The author has done well in expounding the relationship between Islam and democracy. The Islamic government, as provided for by the Quran and the sunnah, does not include a specific form of constitutional system. What the texts rather do is lay down the basic principles on which any constitution can be based. The ruler must be chosen by others and may rule only in accordance with the law. The affairs of the community have to be managed by majority decisions, which is the essence of the *shura* system. The Prophet, in his capacity as head of the Islamic state, was bound by the shura system in so far as his actions were not dictated by divine revelation. As to how shura was exercised in practice, i.e. all matters of form, they were left to be determined in accordance with the needs and circumstances of each time and place. Thus the vital element of flexibility was guaranteed. To draw a little more on the history of Omar's caliphate, he normally used to conduct shura in the mosque. When the subject matter was difficult and required much deliberation, he took to an open space outside of town along with all the participants in the consultations. There they would spend days on end, discussing the matter until they could reach a majority decision by which the ruler would be bound.

In addition to majority rule in accordance with the shura system, Islam firmly established the concept of human rights. Freedom of worship, speech and movement, and equality between citizens of the state, were all safeguarded, long before other nations began the tortuous route towards introducing them into their systems. Unfortunately, much has changed since the dawn of Islam and many of the pristine features of the Islamic constitutional system have been allowed to erode away. In some Islamic states, one cannot avoid the impression that there is a definite antipathy between Islam and democracy.

The author has given a clear and succinct explanation of the five pillars of Islam, which a Muslim normally learns during childhood. This object is to give the non-Muslim reader a clear picture of how a Muslim strives towards perfection in his relationship with his Creator, in the matters of worship and in observing God's commands and prohibitions in his daily conduct. It is this latter part of the Muslim's life, i.e. his or her behavior or conduct towards others, which most readily catches the observer's attention. Here the moral standard set by Islam is high and pervades all aspects of life, making the true Muslim generous, tolerant, and modest, striving to do good unto his fellow Muslims as much as he would do unto his own kith and kin. The author cites brilliant examples from the Quran and the sunnah that have influenced Muslims over the centuries and are capable of giving the non-Muslim a vivid picture of what Islam is all about.

The fifth and final chapter concerns political and social issues about which there is much controversy throughout the world. The author's views and proposed solutions are a reflection of his deep understanding of the Islamic Shari'ah and the moral principles that it introduced. Some Muslims may beg to differ with the author's theories or conclusions. Such difference of opinion, however, is welcomed by Islam, and the rule that our Prophet laid down for us in this respect is that "he who exerts his mind in quest of the truth or the solution to a point in issue and finds the right answer shall win two rewards, whereas he who exerts his mind and misses the truth shall gain one reward." To my mind Dr. Hathout's efforts, choosing as he does to look for the spirit and wisdom of the texts rather than only their literal meaning, will gain him two rewards, not one.

# Preface

I was born in Egypt during the time of the British occupation. This played quite a role in my life, since the earliest of my early memories as a little child was my mother's prodding time after time, "When I was carrying you I made a pledge to call you Hassan and devote you to expelling the British from Egypt." That registered with me quite powerfully. The result? No carefree childhood and no delinquent adolescence. There was a cause, and a purpose in life!

My generation followed in the footsteps of previous generations in combating the British occupation by whatever means necessary. To the British and their surrogate Egyptian governments we were terrorists, to the rest of the country and the world we were freedom fighters. We were lucky to see the end of the British occupation. When I later lived in Britain to pursue my studies, I acquired love and admiration for the British people. I realized that people can be very different from the foreign policy of their politicians and statesmen. The same also happened to me much later, when I came to America to make it my home.

Seriousness and resolve fueled my scholastic life. I sailed through my higher clinical qualifications in obstetrics and gynecology, and to ensure a solid academic base I obtained my Ph.D. from the University of Edinburgh, Scotland; my thesis was "Studies in Normal and Abnormal Human Embryogenesis." I had the satisfaction of achieving my life dream of becoming a university professor, chairman of my department, clinician, scientist and teacher, and of attaining high standing in my professional circles regionally, nationally, and internationally.

All this, however, was only one of my two lungs with which to breathe. My other love was the study of religion, primarily my own but others also. My readings were no less extensive than those of formal students of religion, but my background in science and medicine provided me with an invaluable tool by which to ponder my religion, understand it, and explain it.

Being bicultural and bilingual, I realized that Islam is very widely known in the West for what it is not (and sometimes I feel that Muslims themselves ought to take part of the blame for this). Active slandering and tarnishing of Islam has become a mission and a career of some groups in politics, the media and the entertainment field.

I strongly believe that it is a basic human right to be known for what one is. I also believe that peace, harmony and goodwill between people can be based only on correct understanding and not on myth or falsehood. People will then become aware of true similarities and differences, and hopefully respect their differences and agree to tolerate and live with them.

This book is a humble contribution in that direction on behalf of the religion of Islam, the faith of one billion of our neighbors on this planet.

I present it in LOVE.
Love is from God.  Hate is from the Devil.

*Hassan Hathout*

Chapter One

# GOD?

I asked my granddaughter, "Do you believe in God?" She almost snapped "Of course!" and then, catching her breath, she added, "Mummy says so!" But then I picked up one of her books and asked her, "Who wrote this book?" and immediately she read the name of the author. Continuing the argument, I said, "Suppose I tear out the front page bearing the name of the author and suggest to you that this book has written itself by itself, without a writer; what would you say?" Her reply was of course an emphatic "Impossible," and the rest of our discussion smoothly and logically established that as a book is proof of a writer, similarly the creation is proof of the Creator.

Straight and simple, but it is a central idea in the thinking of a Muslim. It was perhaps a similar intellectual process that led the patriarch Abraham (also known in Islam as the father of the prophets) to find God. Convinced of the falsity of the idols his people carved and worshipped, he started to consider articles of nature for godhood, such as the stars, moon, and sun, only to find that all were obedient to certain laws; so he pondered on the One who set those laws. The Quranic account of this is most interesting:

*So also did We show Abraham the realm of the heavens and earth, that he might have certitude.*

*When the night covered him over he saw a star. He said, "This is my Lord," but when it set, he said, "I love not those that set." When he saw the moon rising in splendor he said, "This is my Lord," but when the moon set he said, "Unless my Lord guides me, I shall surely be among those who go astray." When he saw the sun rising in splendor, he said "This is my Lord, this is the greatest." But when the sun set, he said, "O my people....I am indeed free from your (guilt of) giving partners (to the One True God). For me, I have set my face firmly and truly toward Him who created the heavens and the earth, and never shall I give partners to Him." (6:75-78)*

Yet, the idea of God is not as popular as one might imagine.  I was surprised to find that many of my scientist colleagues in the academic circles of America and Europe, and not just from the ex-communist bloc, were atheist.  I myself tried hard to be one at a stage of my life.  It was in vogue at one time just after the Second World War, among university students in my mother country of Egypt.  I did try to conform with my peers but could never apply myself to the concept of a Godless universe.  The issue was finally laid to rest when one evening I opened the dictionary to look up the meaning of a word and an idea dawned on me:  suppose someone had suggested to me that the unerring arrangement of the words in the dictionary was the outcome of an explosion in a printer's shop, which caused the lead letters to be blown up in the air and then fall, just like that, in alphabetical order, the way they are in the dictionary.  My mind just couldn't take it!

If He is the Ultimate Creator, it follows that nothing could be "more" than Him in any respect, or else He would be "less" than something, He would have limits, and that would be incompatible with being the Ultimate One or the Primary Cause that philosophy refers to. His dimensions in all His attributes can be expressed in terms of infinity. The science of mathematics does indeed acknowledge infinity as a mathematical fact and expresses it with a special sign. Of course, we cannot comprehend what infinity really means, but we should acknowledge that this is only natural, since we are finite, and the finite cannot comprehend the infinite. God therefore can comprehend us and though we, by our finitude, cannot comprehend Him, we know about Him by knowing His signs and manifestations through His creation. And since infinity cannot be divided by two or three or more (a mathematical fact), it follows that there cannot be one God for Jews, another for Christians, another for Muslims, another for Hindus and yet another for the godless, etcetera. God is One! It is this Oneness of God that is at the root of the Islamic faith and the belief of Muslims.

When the pronoun "He" is used to refer to God, of course it carries no gender connotations. God is beyond such classification and the question is one of linguistic usage, which is both limited and arbitrary. Speaking of languages, it is noteworthy that some languages (including English) do not have a word by which to signify the One Ultimate Creator; therefore, the capitalization of the word *God* is necessary in order to distinguish it from other (man made) gods that are signified by a lowercase "g". Other languages reserve a special name for Him. It is *Allah* in the Arabic language. Whether one reads *God* (English), *Dieu* (French), *Adonai* (Hebrew), or *Allah* (Arabic), there should be no confusion. Quite often I have been asked by audiences at my talks, "If you worship God, then who is Allah?" At other times the reference is not as innocent, since some scholars who know better teach that Muslims do not worship God and have a separate god of their own whom they call Allah!

# Chapter Two

# SO WHAT?

## THE CREED OF ISLAM

**God is.**

Some will ask, "So what?" Should we really bother whether God is or is not, or is the question merely an academic one, attracting only the interest of theologians and philosophical theoreticians? What is the relevance of the existence or nonexistence of God and the practical implications of His existence (or nonexistence) for human society?

Assuming God is, and that He is the Ultimate Creator, a study of His creation immediately shows that we human beings stand out in clear distinction from the rest of the creation that we have so far been able to study. From atom to galaxy, all are obedient to the laws governing them. Our constituent atoms and molecules are the same as those in nature and, inside us, obey the same laws. As they become more complex and form nucleic acid (the self-replicating molecule which is the basic ingredient of life), chemistry merges with biology, which also obeys its own laws. In this respect we are astonishingly similar to higher animals.

When I was at school we were taught that Man (generic for men and women) was the head of the animal kingdom. Yet, somehow we do not recognize ourselves as animals. Although we share biology with animals in terms of having systems of circulation, respiration, digestion, metabolism, immunity, locomotion, sensation, reproduction, etcetera, we also know that it is not our biology that makes us human beings. Amongst all the species we have studied, we alone are the species that has gone beyond biology. We are suprabiologic beings for whom biology is not the ultimate guide of behavior. We have the same instincts and drives, but whereas animals simply respond to these in a simple one-step fashion, our response is regulated by a complex mechanism that goes beyond inherent programming. We may share our biology with animals, but we have definitely ventured beyond biology into the realm of values, principles and spirituality. Indeed, it is true to say that we are spiritual creatures housed in biological containers (our bodies). Those of us whose concern in life is to cater to the needs (and greeds) of their biological component and who fall short of the spiritual might well be described as animals, at least figuratively.

Studying man, we realize that the Creator has endowed us with four cardinal features that are unique to our species: knowledge, an awareness of good and evil, freedom of choice, and accountability:

*Knowledge.* We have a love of knowledge and seek to acquire more and more of it. Our brain is equipped to observe, imagine, rationalize, analyze, experiment and conclude. We yearn to know the past and future and to decipher nature in and around us, and we record and express our knowledge in various ways.

*An awareness of good and evil.* We would be simplistic to expect good to always be attractive and evil repulsive.  The complexity of human life, the suggestibility of the human mind and its inclination to rationalization, and the fact that evil might be very tempting, certainly may confound the picture, but our awareness of good and evil is an inherent part of our being.

*Freedom of choice.*  Our freedom of choice stems from the "autonomy" with which the Creator has endowed our species.  Obviously this freedom is not absolute and extends to a limited sphere beyond which it ceases to operate.  Yet, within this sphere, freedom is a cardinal value that is of supreme importance in human life.

*Accountability.*  It is the freedom of choice which is the premise for man's accountability.  We innately realize that we are accountable and bear responsibility for our choices.  This is not an invention of religion, for even in an atheist society if you break the traffic lights you will be fined.  Within the realm of religion, accountability implies that unless one is free, one should not face judgment or the Day of Judgment.  Freedom is therefore the core and essence of being human, both from a religious and a secular perspective.  God created a species that will bear responsibility for its actions; therefore, God created a species whose hallmark is freedom.  Events that are beyond our sphere of choice or capacity to influence are a matter of "fate," and, of course, we cannot be held accountable for them.

We are therefore the species that leads a life of continual self-debate and continual decision making. Quite often we emotionally vacillate between what we know is right and what we know is wrong and have to resort to our will power and our faculty of self-restraint when indicated, or else we fall into wrong and must face the consequences of our acts. Animals are exempt from this continuous battle within the self; without blame, they simply respond to whatever they feel like doing. Scriptures tell us that angels do only good, but that is because they are not capable of evil. The others respond to programming, we respond to choice. This is indeed the nobility of humanity. It explains why God, according to the scriptures, ordered the angels to bow to Adam, although they are immune to sin and Adam is not, and they obeyed Him.

Let us digress a bit here and consider the universe and man. The more we scientifically study the universe, the more we realize that we live in a universe of equations so delicately balanced that the slightest imbalance would lead to a cosmic catastrophe.

Now we look at human societies and see people who live their full lives in what we call wrong, evil or sin, seem to thoroughly enjoy it, and at the end, die. Others, by contrast, spend their lives struggling for truth, fighting for justice and suffering in the cause of their ideals, and finally they die. Can that be all? Can death be the ultimate end to both kinds of life? Something in our innermost being refuses to accept it. Where then is man's accountability? If death were the end of the story, then human life would be in conflict with that delicate balance that pervades the whole universe. The only conclusion, therefore, is that death *cannot* be the end. Death cannot be followed by void, but by another life in which balance is restored and accountability fulfilled. This is the hereafter that religions tell about, when people will be judged by God, the Ultimate Judge, on the Day of Judgment.

God grants us autonomy and holds us in account-ability. We are not perfect creatures, nor were we meant to be. We are required to do our best in the face of difficulty and temptation, and often our "best" is not foolproof. We strive, and our life is a perpetual battle. It is reasonable, therefore, that God acknowl-edges our endeavor, appreciates our striving and loves us as His noblest creature. He would certainly love to see us pass the test of accountability, our freedom of choice notwithstanding. The best way to do that is to keep us reminded of Him as Ultimate Resort and Lord, of what is good and evil as He delineates them to us, and of the inevitable Day of Judgment, when we will be held accountable. This He has done by select-ing certain members of the human family, contacting them in His own way (eg. direct talk, written tablets, inspiration or through an angel) and giving them the assignment of carrying His message to their fellow humans: worship God and only God, do good and refrain from evil, and always remember your inevitable accountability before Him on the inescapable Day of Judgment. This is the concept of prophethood, and throughout history humanity received a large number of prophets and messengers. Of this long chain, some God mentioned by name in the scriptures, some He gave scriptures, and others He gave the power to per-form specific miracles. The last three major prophets in this chain are the principal personalities of the Abrahamic monotheistic religions of Judaism, Christianity, and Islam. These three figures are all descendants of the patriarch Abraham, Muhammad by

way of Ishmael, and Moses and Jesus by way of Isaac
(Ishmael and Isaac were the two sons of Abraham).

It is appropriate at this juncture, however, to point
out that for Jews the line of prophets stops with
Judaism.  To them Jesus was not the Messiah, nor was
his mother, Mary, the chaste woman she claimed she
was.   They still await the Messiah and deny
Christianity as a divine religion.  For Christians, the
line ends with Christianity, although they acknowledge
Judaism as a divine religion (without reciprocity on
the part of the Jews).  Islam, on the other hand, recognizes both Judaism and Christianity as religions based
on divine revelation, in spite of the fact that neither
Jews nor Christians believe Islam to be so, nor do they
believe that Muhammad was a true prophet and messenger of God.  It is part of the faith of every Muslim
(the person who professes Islam) to believe in Moses
and Jesus and the scriptures revealed to them, and to
believe in the preceding line of prophets.  Indeed in
the Quran, the scripture of Islam that Muslims believe
to be the very word of God, Muslims read:

> *The same religion has He established for you as that*
> *which He enjoined on Noah, that which We revealed*
> *unto you, and that which We enjoined on Abraham,*
> *Moses and Jesus: that you should steadfastly uphold*
> *the faith and break not your unity therein.* (42:13)

A short briefing about the Quran would be of help
to non-Muslim readers before moving on.  The Quran,
Muslims believe, is the recorded word of God Himself,
verbatim and literally, and was conveyed as such to
Prophet Muhammad by the angel Gabriel.  In its com-

pletion, it is a book approximately the size of the New Testament, but it was not revealed all at once. It came in short passages addressing various topics and commenting on issues and incidents, and its revelation was completed over the span of twenty-three years.

Whenever Prophet Muhammad received a segment of the Quran and wanted to convey it to his followers, he indicated the equivalent of quote (") and unquote ("), at the beginning saying "God says" and at the end saying "God spoke the truth." The new verses were immediately committed to the memory of the people as well as written down on the writing materials then available. When the Quran was completed, Muhammad put it in its final arrangement (not necessarily in chronological order but upon divine instruction), and it has been preserved ever since, in its original language and form, word for word and letter for letter. As a scripture the Quran is unique in this respect. Once translated it is no longer called the Quran, but the translation or the meanings thereof, because any translation is human rendering and not the original word of God.

The language of the Quran is Arabic, in which it is considered an inimitable literary miracle. It challenged the Arabs at the time of the Prophet to imitate it, but they could not and were awed by it, although they prided themselves on their literary power. Some of the staunchest enemies of Islam at the time embraced it just upon listening to passages from the Quran.

Chapter Three

# ISLAM AND THE OTHERS

According to the Quran every human being is honored solely by virtue of being human, without any further consideration of race, origin, or creed. The Quran says, *"We have honored the children of Adam, provided them with transport on land and sea, and conferred on them special favors above a great part of our creation"* (17:70).

Islam emphasizes the oneness of humanity as a family: *"O mankind, fear your Guardian Lord, who created you from a single self and created—out of it— its mate, and made from them twain scattered (like seeds) countless men and women"* (4:1). All people equally possess basic human rights, including the right to freely choose one's religion without coercion, for within Islam the space of the "other" is well-preserved and protected. Islam is not an exclusive religion, and no human being, clergy or otherwise, is permitted to set limits on God's mercy and forgiveness, or to speak on His behalf in assigning reward or punishment. The ultimate judge is God Himself: *"Your return in the end is toward Allah. . .He will tell you the truth of the things wherein you disputed"* (6:164).

## THE PEOPLE OF THE BOOK
**(Jews and Christians)**

From amongst humanity, Jews and Christians are the nearest to Muslims and are given the honorary title of *People of the Book*. They are fellow believers in the One God and the recipients of scriptures from Him. They share the belief in the line of prophethood, and many of our Jewish and Christian friends are taken by surprise when they learn that the biblical prophets are also Islamic prophets. The three religions share a common moral code. The Quran says,

> *Say: 'We believe in God, and the revelation given to us, and the revelation given to Abraham, Ishmael, Isaac, Jacob and the Tribes, and that given to Moses and Jesus, and that given to (all) the prophets from their Lord: We make no distinction between one and another of them, and to Him we are submitters.'* (2:136)

The word *Islam* literally means "submission to the will of God."

Muslims are permitted by Islam to eat the food offered them by the People of the Book (unless specifically prohibited, such as alcohol or pork) and to reciprocate by offering their food to them: *"The food of the People of the Book is lawful unto you and your food is lawful unto them"* (5:5). Further, a Muslim man is permitted to take in marriage (the most intimate relation and sacred bond) a Jewish or Christian woman: *"Lawful unto you in marriage are (not only) chaste women who are believers, but chaste women among the People of the Book revealed before your time when you give them their due dowers and desire chastity, and not lewdness, taking them as lovers"* (5:5). In such a situation it is unlawful for the Muslim husband to try to exert pressure on his wife to convert to Islam, because that would contradict the Quranic injunction, *"Let there be no compulsion in religion"* (2:256). It would indeed be his Islamic duty to ensure her right of worship according to her own faith.

In an Islamic state the legal dictum about the People of the Book is that "they have our rights and owe our duties." They are equally eligible for social security and other benefits the state provides. Muslims were warned against acts of bigotry or prejudice towards the People of the Book, and Prophet Muhammad himself said, "Whoever hurts a person from the People of the Book, it will be as though he hurt me personally."

As a matter of fact, from its inception the Islamic society was a pluralistic society. As soon as Muhammad immigrated to Madinah to establish the earliest Islamic state, a treaty was concluded between all the tribes, including the Jewish tribes who lived there, establishing religious freedom and equal rights and duties.

Islam is not an exclusive religion. It is a universal call to mankind (not an "Arab" or an "Eastern" religion as many depict it). Although it addresses all people, including the People of the Book, their failure to embrace it is no reason to categorize them as enemies or infidels. As a matter of fact the term "infidel" is of European origin, used at the time of the Crusades to describe Muslims.

Goodness is acknowledged by Islam wherever it resides: *"Not all of them are alike: of the People of the Book are a portion that stand (for the right); they rehearse the signs of God all night long and they prostrate themselves in adoration"* (3:113). No individual or group can claim monopoly of God's mercy or deny it to others: *"Those who believe (in the Quran), and those who follow the Jewish (scriptures), and the Christians, and the Sabians, any who believe in God and the Last Day, and work righteousness, shall have their reward with their Lord, on them shall be no fear, nor shall they grieve"* (2:62).

## DOCTRINAL DIFFERENCES

The commonalities that Islam shares with Judaism and Christianity are vast and its reality is very different from the stereotype that is held by a major segment of the population in the West. Islam, in fact, is nearer to both Christianity and Judaism than they are to each other, since it recognizes both as religions based upon divine revelation, whereas the Jews recognize neither Christianity nor Islam as such. In this respect it would seem that the term "Judeo-Christian" is a misnomer, and in my opinion it was coined, politically, for the sole purpose of excluding Muslims. A more appropriate description of our current civilization would be Judeo-Christian-Islamic, in that the three religions are rooted in the Abrahamic tradition and the civilization of the Islamic era furnished the foundation for the present civilization. It was a civilization in which Muslims,

Jews, Christians, and others lived in safety and justice under a system of tolerance and cooperation.

Vast as the commonalities might be, it is beneficial to also be aware of doctrinal differences that exist between Islam and the other communities of the Abrahamic faiths. A general outline will be given with no intention whatsoever of confrontation or attacking other faiths, but to enable Jewish and Christian readers to clarify and reappraise their position towards Islam, rather than continuing to malign it out of ignorance and misunderstanding, which underlies much of the existing animosity and ill will.

Foremost of these differences, perhaps, is how Muslims perceive God and express themselves towards Him. God is the eternal, the infinite and the absolute in all His attributes. It is beyond us to imagine a form for Him or define Him in any way that portrays Him as limited or as less than the infinite being He is. The most reverent language is used when referring to God. It is therefore alien to the Muslim mind to read (in the Bible) that God walked in the Garden of Eden, or that He assembled the angels and said to them about Adam *"Behold, the man is become as one of us,"* or that He regretted His own decision and action (after the flood), saying, "I wish I had not done it," or that God worked for six days and then had to rest on the seventh, or that anyone wrestled with God and almost defeated Him.

Another aspect concerns prophets and messengers appointed by God. Muslims believe that these were handpicked by God, both to convey His message and to be role models for their communities. Whenever societies slipped back into idol worship or associated partners with God or deviated from the moral code ordained by Him, prophets and messengers were sent to remind and correct the course. If human perfection were ever tenable, they would be its epitome and embodiment. The idea that God's prophets committed serious transgressions against His laws, as depicted in biblical portrayals of them cheating and committing carnal sin (such as Jacob's supposed betrayal of his brother, and Lot's supposedly having committed incest with his daughters while drunk), is at complete variance with Islamic teachings. The only conclusion open to Muslims is that such depictions of the prophets resulted from human interpolation into the scriptures.

## THE JEWS

Muslims often refer to the Jews as their cousins, since Abraham was the common grandfather of Muhammad by way of Ishmael, and Israel (Jacob) and his children by way of Isaac. As is well known, Abraham's marriage to Sarah was barren until she was well advanced in age. Before the birth of Sarah's son, Isaac, Abraham had married Hagar, who conceived and gave birth to Ishmael. According to the Quran, as a test for Abraham and as a fulfillment of God's plan, God ordered Abraham to take his only son, Ishmael, to the place that, centuries later, became the city of Makkah, where the prophet Muhammad would eventually be born. The anguish of Hagar searching for water for her son after their provisions were exhausted, and the unexpected eruption of the well of Zam-

Zam, is commemorated annually by Muslims amongst
the rituals of *hajj* (pilgrimage), and when visiting the
Kaaba, the first mosque, built for the worship of the
One God, erected by Abraham and Ishmael. God
willed that Sarah also, well into her menopause, would
conceive and give birth to Isaac, the father of Jacob,
whose name was later changed to Israel, the father of
the twelve Children of Israel.

Muslims are somewhat dismayed that large seg-
ments of Jews and Christians do not consider Ishmael
to be Abraham's legitimate son, since the biblical version depicts Hagar as Abraham's wife as well as
Sarah's maid (Genesis 16:3). In my copy of the King
James Version[1] the name of Ishmael is altogether miss-
ing from the glossary, and I was able to retrieve his
story only by using Abraham as my key. Time and
again Genesis (16:16; 17:23, 25, 26; 21:11) refers to
Ishmael as "his [Abraham's] son," thus making it
impossible to deny that sonhood. Moreover, tracing
the maternal side of the Children of Israel, Genesis
tells us that Israel married his two cousins, Rachel and
Leah, and their two maids, Zilpah and Bilhah, and out
of the four of them came the twelve Children of Israel.
Yet no one has ever claimed that any of them were less
the Children of Israel because their mothers were
maids! Is there a double standard set against Ishmael?
In regard to the account in Genesis 22:2, which states
that God said to Abraham, *"Take now thy son, thine
only son Isaac, whom thou lovest, and get thee into the
land of Moriah, and offer him there for a burnt offering
upon one of the mountains which I will tell thee of,"*

---

[1] Authorized King James Version, Great Britain: Collins World, 1975.

Muslims feel that the mention of Isaac's name was deliberately inserted, for at no time was Isaac the only son of Abraham, being (according to Genesis 17:24-26) thirteen years younger than Ishmael, and both sons being alive when their father died.

The commemoration of this trying test of Abraham, his submission to God, and his willingness to slay his only son (Ishmael), is annually commemorated by Muslims as one of the rituals of hajj (pilgrimage). To Muslims, however, both Ishmael and Isaac are equally blessed and beloved prophets.

The Quran makes some fifty references to Jews or the Children of Israel, apart from mentioning Moses some 137 times and the Torah eighteen times. Generous praise was heaped upon them, as well as a fair share of blame and rebuke. Examples are:

> *O children of Israel, call to mind the favor which I bestowed on you, and that I preferred you to all others. Then guard yourselves against a day when one soul shall not avail another, nor shall intercession be accepted for it, nor shall compensation be taken from it, nor shall anyone be helped (from outside). And remember, We delivered you from the people of the Pharaoh: they set you hard tasks and chastisement, slaughtered your sons and let your womenfolk live; therein was tremendous trial from your Lord. And remember We parted the sea for you and saved you and drowned Pharaoh's people within your very sight. And remember We appointed forty nights for Moses, and in his absence you took the calf (for worship) and you did grievous wrong. Even then We did forgive you; there was a chance for you to be grateful. (2:47-52)*

*We settled the Children of Israel in an honorable dwelling place, and provided for them sustenance of the best: it was after knowledge had been granted to them that they fell into schisms. Verily God will judge between them as to the schisms amongst them on the Day of Judgment.* (10:93)

It is to be noted that whenever the Quran rebukes the Jews, it is in fact because they did something that the Quran deems in conflict with their religion (the Bible also, in several passages, calls the Jews to account for disobedience to God [see, for example, 2 Kings 17:7-23]). The Quran, however, does not condemn the Jews as a people, or denigrate or laud any ethnic group or race. In fact the Quran gives due consideration to the fact that for a long period of time the Jews were the only bearers of monotheism in a world that was pagan or idolatrous. With the arrival of Christianity and Islam, however, the claim of the Jews to have the sole monopoly of monotheism loses its ground, and with it the concept of the chosen race that they cling to until today. At least this is what Christians and Muslims feel.

Islam does not subscribe to the concept of a chosen race. God says in the Quran:

*You Mankind: We have created you from a single pair of a male and a female, and made you into nations and tribes that you might come to know and cherish one another (not to despise one another). Verily the most honorable of you in the sight of God are the most righteous.* (49:13)

People can become better or worse only on the basis of righteousness, not by virtue of belonging to a particular ancestral line. This is vividly expressed in the Quranic version of God's promise to Abraham:

> And remember that Abraham was tried by his Lord
> with certain commands which he fulfilled: He said,
> "I will make thee an imam (leader) to the people."
> He pleaded, "And also (imams) from my offspring!"
> He (God) answered, "But My promise is not within
> the reach of evil-doers." (2:124)

The conflict between Arabs and Jews today stems from a myopic emphasis upon the biblical version of the Covenant given by God to Abraham: *"And I will give unto thee, and to thy seed after thee, the land wherein thou art a stranger, all the land of Canaan for an everlasting possession"* (Gen. 17:8). The complexity of the Palestinian problem derives from the belief of the Jews that the "seed of Abraham" includes only the Jews. Accordingly, much of contemporary Judaism believes that only Jews have a right to live in the land that, less than a century ago, was populated primarily by Muslim and Christian Palestinians, who coexisted peacefully with a small Jewish minority. Later, the majority of those Palestinians were actually forced to leave their homes and land by the Zionists who founded the contemporary state of Israel.[2] Further, the Children of Israel who have converted to Christianity or Islam are automatically excluded from the current

---

[2] For a moving biographical account of this, see Elias Chacour's *Blood Brothers* (Grand Rapids: Chosen Books, 1984).

Israeli "law of return," although they are legitimate descendants of Israel (i.e., Prophet Jacob, the son of Isaac, the son of Abraham, or the first son of Abraham, Ishmael). Neither they nor the Palestinian Muslims and Christians view themselves as outsiders who must either leave or live as second-class citizens in their land, the land of their ancestors for millennia. They can hardly swallow such statements as Golda Meir's, "There is no such thing as the Palestinians, they do not exist,"[3] or that of Joseph Weitz, former head of the Jewish National Fund: "Between ourselves it must be clear that there is no room for both peoples together in this country."[4]

Muslims do not view the Palestinian problem as a fight between religions, but as a conflict between two groups of people with different rationale and objectives. Its resolution, according to all three of the Abrahamic religions, requires an attempt at a peaceful solution. A truly peaceful solution is one based upon justice and fairness, which is the only assurance of its permanency. A peaceful solution is far from being a negotiated resultant between the powerful and the weak. A Versailles mentality should not dominate the negotiations, but it takes farsighted statesmanship to realize this.

We believe that this part of the world should be the converging and not the diverging site for the three Abrahamic faiths to manifest the spirit of tolerance and Godliness, celebrating the unity that encompasses their diversity. Both common sense and religion point in that

---

[3] *Sunday Times* (London), 1969, 15 June. Quoted in R. Garaudy, *The Case of Israel* (London: Shorouk International, 1983), 37.

[4] *Davar* (Israel). 1967, 29 September.

direction if only all sides would open their ears and hearts to the voice of God.

Historically, the relation between Muslims and Jews has had its fluctuations, but never because Islam harbored animosity to Judaism as a faith. Conflict was situational and based upon justifiable reasons. However, we should be far from claiming that the history of Muslims has always been a true representation of the teachings of Islam. Particularly under dictatorial rule, Jews and Christians have had their share of maltreatment, but this was not to the exclusion of the Muslim subjects, who were always indeed the most to suffer. In the Muslim world Jews never suffered anything like the atrocities inflicted on them by Christian Europe over the centuries, including the holocaust in this century. It was in Christendom that the Jews were branded as killers of God and made to pay for it through one pogrom after another. Even when the enemy was Muslims, Europe always included the Jews as "collateral damage." The first Crusade was launched by the massacre of thousands of Jews in Europe, with this mischievous rationalization: "We have set out to march a long way to fight the enemies of God in the East, and behold before our very eyes are his worst foes, the Jews. They must be dealt with first."[5]

In 1492, the Jews were expelled from Spain as a result of the victory of Ferdinand and Isabella over the Muslims. Contrary to previous promises, it was made illegal for Muslims or Jews to practice their religion; they were condemned to death or expulsion if they did

---

[5] Cohn, Norman. *The Pursuit of the Millennium.* Quoted in Bamber Gascoigne, *The Christians* (London: Jonathan Cape, 1977), 113.

not convert to Catholicism. Many Jews chose to go to Turkey, then the seat of the Islamic Caliphate, and were generously received, the Sultan mocking Ferdinand and Isabella's expulsion of the Jews by saying, "They impoverished their kingdom and enriched mine." The Muslim era in Spain was one during which the Jewish contribution to civilization particularly flourished. Perhaps the most famous example of this is the great Maimonides, who was the student of the Islamic philosopher Ibn Rushd (Averroes) of Cordova, and later, when he moved to Egypt, he was the personal physician of Salahuddin (Saladin, of Crusades fame).

In his book, *My People*[6] (also produced as a TV series), Mr. Abba Eban, Israeli scholar, historian and former foreign secretary, stated that the Jews had in two episodes during their history been treated justly, once in Muslim Spain and the second, currently, in the United States of America. Over the centuries, the Jewish citizens of Islamic countries have enjoyed security and prosperity. Until this day many Islamic countries house sizable Jewish communities who, in spite of the agonizing repercussions of the Palestinian problem, fare no worse than their Muslim and Christian compatriots.

## THE CHRISTIANS

*"Relate in the Book (the story of) Mary, when she withdrew from her family to a place in the East. She placed a screen (to conceal herself) from them: then*

---

[6] Ebban, Abba. *My People.* New York: Behrman, 1968.

*We sent to her Our angel, and he appeared before
her as a man in all respects. She said: 'I seek refuge
from you with Allah (God) Most Gracious: (come
not near) if you fear Allah.' He said 'Nay, I am only
a messenger from your Lord (to announce) to you
the gift of a pure son.' She said: 'How shall I have a
son whereas no man has touched me, and I am not
unchaste?' He said: 'So (it will be): your Lord said,
"It is easy for Me: and (We wish) to appoint him as
a sign unto people and a mercy from Us" . . .it is a
matter (so) decreed.'*

*So she conceived him, and she retired with him to a
remote place. And the pains of childbirth drove her
to the trunk of a palm tree. She cried (in her
anguish), 'Ah! would that I had died before this . . .
would that I had been a thing forgotten.' But a voice
called to her from beneath (the palm tree): 'Grieve
not! Your Lord has provided a rivulet beneath you;
and shake toward yourself the trunk of the palm tree
and it will let fall upon you fresh ripe dates. So eat
and drink and cool your eye. And if you see any
human (person), say 'I have vowed a fast to God
Most Gracious, so this day I will enter into no talk
with any human being.'*

*At length she brought the babe to her people, carrying
him (in her arms) and they said, 'O Mary! You have
indeed done an amazing thing. O Sister of Aaron:
Your father was not a man of evil nor your mother a
woman unchaste!' But she pointed to the babe and
they said, 'How can we talk to one who is a child in the
cradle?' He (the babe) said: 'I am indeed a servant of*

*Allah (God); He has given me Revelation and made
me a prophet. And He has made me blessed whereso-
ever I be; and has enjoined on me prayers and zakah
(alms-giving) as long as I live. And made me kind to
my mother and not overbearing or unblessed. So
peace be on me the day I was born, the day I die, and
the day I shall be raised up to life (again).'"* (19:16-33)

Such is one narration of the story of Jesus in the
Quran. The Quran mentions him as "Jesus" twenty-
five times, as the "Messiah" eleven times, and as only
the "Son of Mary" twice. Mary is mentioned by name
thirty-four times and as *"the one who guarded her
chastity"* twice. Muslims are astounded and dumb-
founded when they read notable scholars, specialists
and, most painful of all, clergy, portraying Islam and
Muslims as the enemies of Christ. Conversely, many
uninformed and misinformed Christians are astonished when we tell them about the respect and love we
have for Jesus and Mary, even though we have doctrinal differences. A few quotations should be sufficient
to express the high esteem in which Jesus and Mary
are regarded in Islam.

*Behold! the angels said: "O Mary: God gives you
glad tidings of a Word from Him: his name will be
Christ Jesus, the son of Mary, held in honor in this
world and the hereafter."* (3:45)

*Christ Jesus, the son of Mary, was the messenger of
God and His Word that He bestowed on Mary and a
Spirit proceeding from Him.* (4:171)

*And (remember) her who guarded her chastity: We*
*breathed into her from Our spirit, and We made her*
*and her son a sign for all peoples.* (21:91)

A principal and obvious difference between the
Jews and Christians is their stand on Jesus, who
Muslims believe was a true and genuine messenger of
God to his fellow Jews. The Quran says "*O you who
believe, be the helpers to (the cause of) God, as said
Jesus the son of Mary to the disciples, 'Who will be my
helpers (to the work of God)?' Said the disciples, 'We
are God's helpers.' Then a portion of the Children of
Israel believed and a portion disbelieved*" (61:14).

Those who rejected Jesus and accused his mother
of unchastity are rebuked by the Quran time and
again: "*. . .they uttered against Mary a grave false
charge, they said (in boast) 'We killed Christ Jesus, son
of Mary, the messenger of God,' . . .But they killed him
not, nor crucified him. . .only a likeness of that was
shown to them, and those who differ therein are full of
doubts with no (certain) knowledge but only conjecture
to follow. For a surety they killed him not: Nay, God
raised him up unto Himself, and God (Allah) is Most
Exalted, Wise*" (4:156-158). Islam, therefore, completely absolved the Jews from Christ's blood. The
view that the one arrested and crucified was other than
Jesus (perhaps Judas Escariot) is held amongst a fac-
tion of Christians. Rebuking the Jews for not accepting Jesus, the Quran says:

*We gave Moses the Book and followed him up with*
*a succession of messengers. We gave Jesus the Son*
*of Mary clear signs and strengthened him with the*

*holy spirit; Is it that whenever there comes to you a*
*messenger with what you do not like, you are puffed*
*up with pride?— some you called impostors and oth-*
*ers you slew.* (2:87)

Muslims believe in the miracles that Jesus performed by God's leave, which the Quran mentions:

> *Then God will say: 'O Jesus Son of Mary:*
> *Remember My favor to you and to your mother.*
> *Behold! I strengthened you with the holy spirit so that*
> *you did speak to the people in childhood and in old*
> *age. Behold! I taught you the Book and Wisdom, the*
> *Torah and the Injil[7]. And behold! you make out of*
> *clay, as it were, the figure of a bird by My leave, and*
> *you breathe into it and it becomes a bird by My leave.*
> *And you heal those born blind and lepers by My*
> *leave. And behold! You bring forth the dead to life*
> *by My leave. And behold! I did restrain the Children*
> *of Israel from you when you showed them the clear*
> *signs: and the unbelievers among them said: "This is*
> *nothing but evident magic."'* (5:110)

The praise widens to encompass also the sincere
followers of Jesus, both early Christians and those at
the time of Prophet Muhammad:

> *Then in their wake (Noah, Abraham and the*
> *prophets from amongst their progeny) We followed*

---

[7] *Injil:* The original book revealed to prophet Jesus (peace be upon
him), which is no longer extant, though portions of it may have survived
in the *Gospel* (or New Testament). Ed.

*them up with (others of) Our messengers: We sent*
*after them Jesus son of Mary, and bestowed on him*
*the Injil, and We ordained in the hearts of those who*
*followed him compassion and mercy.* (57:27)

*And nearest (among people) in love to the believers*
*(Muslims) you will find those who say "We are*
*Christians," because amongst these are priests and monks,*
*and because they are not given to arrogance.* (5:82)

Let us now consider some of the differences between Muslims and Christians. Foremost among these is that Muslims, believing in the chastity of the virgin Mary, say that Jesus was "created" by God without a father, yet do not say "begotten" by God. To them God is beyond such biological characterizations, for He is the eternal and the absolute, as is expressed in the Quran: *"Say: He is Allah (God) the one; Allah, the Eternal, Absolute; He begets not, nor is He begotten; and there is none like unto Him"* (112:1-4). A belief in the literal sonhood of Jesus to God is at variance with the Islamic faith (although it is acceptable to say that, metaphorically, we are all the children of God).

Also unacceptable is the doctrine that Mary is the mother of God. Both Mary and Jesus are human beings highly honored by Islam, and the fact that Jesus was born without a father does not, according to Islamic doctrine, make him "the only begotten son of God." The Quran relates, *"The similitude of Jesus before God is as that of Adam; He created him from dust, then said to him: 'Be': and he was"* (3:59).

According to the Quran, Jesus never claimed divinity for himself or for his mother:

*And behold! Allah will say, "O Jesus son of Mary:*
*did you say unto the people 'Take me and my moth-*
*er for two gods besides Allah?' He will say 'Glory to*
*You. Never could I say what I had no right (to say).*
*Had I said such a thing you would indeed have*
*known it. You know what is in my heart though I*
*don't know what is in Yours, for You know in full*
*all that is hidden. Never said I to them aught except*
*what You did command me to say: "Worship Allah,*
*my Lord and your Lord." And I was a witness over*
*them while I dwelt amongst them; when You did take*
*me up You were the Watcher over them, and You are*
*a witness to all things. If You punish them, they are*
*Your servants; if You forgive them, You are indeed*
*the Exalted (in power), the Wise.'"* (5:116-118)

Muslims therefore identify with such verses in the
New Testament as this statement attributed to Jesus:
*"Why callest thou me good? There is none good but*
*One, that is God"* (Mark 10:18).

According to the New Testament, when Jesus was
on the cross he cried, *"Eloi Eloi, lama sabachtani?"*
translated as *"My God, my God, why hast thou forsak-*
*en me?"* (Mark 15:34). Obviously he must have been
talking to someone other than himself. The whole concept of the trinity and of the triune God has no place in
Islam: *"Say not three; desist, it will be better for you, for*
*God is One God, glory be to Him, (far exalted is He)*
*above having a son. To Him belong all things in heav-*
*ens and on earth"* (4:171). Muslims do not conceive
that infinity can be divided or compartmentalized into
three, or accept the deification of Jesus or the Holy
Spirit. We hold that Jesus never said anything about

three divine persons in a "single Godhead" and that his concept of God never differed from that of the earlier prophets who preached the unity (never the trinity) of God. Moreover, the concept of the trinity was unknown to the early Christians. Historically, it was decreed to be the creed of the Roman Empire in the Congress of Nicaea in the year 325 C.E. and was enforced by all the might of the empire under Emperor Constantine. The New Catholic Encyclopedia[8] states: "The formulation 'one God in three persons' was not solidly established into Christian life and its profession of faith, prior to the 4th Century."

Another area of variance is the concept of original sin. According to the Bible, the devil tempted Eve to eat from the forbidden tree, and she then tempted Adam to do the same: thus committing the sin. They were then punished by being banished in shame to Planet Earth, with more blame befalling Eve as the prime perpetrator: *"Unto the woman He said: I will greatly multiply thy sorrow and thy conception; in sorrow thou shalt bring forth children, and thy desire shall be to thy husband and he shall rule over thee"* (Genesis 3:16). The common Christian teaching is that all human beings inherit that sin, and that every newborn is born in sin.

In the Quranic version of this event the devil tempted both Adam and Eve, they both sinned, they both repented, they both were forgiven, and that was the end of the original sin: *"So Satan whispered suggestions to them in order to reveal to them their shame that was hidden from them (before). . . .He said to the*

---

[8] *New Catholic Encyclopedia*, s.v. "The Holy Trinity."

*two of them, 'Your Lord only forbade you this tree lest you become angels or such beings as live forever,' and he swore to them both that he was their sincere advisor"* (7:20-21). After their repentance, *"Adam learnt from his Lord certain words and his Lord forgave him, for He is Oft-Returning, Most Merciful"* (2:37). Adam was then raised to prophethood and the human race was delegated to Planet Earth as God's vicegerent. Satan swore to follow them and corrupt them, but God promised to provide them with such guidance as to immunize them against Satan's plots, except those who willed to turn their backs to divine guidance. Every human being therefore is born pure, and it is only later on that our choices blemish us and make us sinners. Sin, according to Islam, is not something that children inherit from their parents.

In this respect, Islam emphasizes that accountability is individual: *"Whoever receives guidance receives it for his (or her) own benefit, and whoever goes astray does so to his own loss. No bearer of burdens can bear the burden of another"* (17:15). The idea of vicarious sacrifice is therefore alien to Islam, and the claim that Jesus, or anyone else, had to be slain in atonement for human sins, is unacceptable. God's forgiveness, in Islam, is to be sought through sincere repentance and doing righteousness, without need for bloodshed. Salvation is granted by the grace of God: *"And those who, having done an act of indecency or wronged their own souls, remember God and ask for forgiveness for their sins— and who can forgive sins except God?—and never knowingly persist in the sin they have done: for such, the reward is forgiveness from their Lord. . ."* (3:135).

No sin is too great for God's forgiveness. *"Say, O My servants who have transgressed against their own selves: despair not of the mercy of God, for God forgives all sins, for He is Oft-Forgiving, Most-Merciful"* (39:53). According to Prophet Muhammad, God says: *"You child of Adam, you approach me with an earthful of sins, then you repent and worship me, taking no associates with Me, and I approach you with an earthful of forgiveness."*

Devoid of the concept of atonement for sin by the blood of Jesus and of the concept of a chosen race (enjoying special privileges with God), Muslims' great hope in God's forgiveness is expressed by being themselves forgivers. The role of forgiveness, whether between individuals, tribes or nations, is of the essence of Islam. Even when the law intervenes by meting out a punishment commensurate with an aggression, the wronged party is encouraged to forgive: *"The recompense for an injury is an injury equal thereto (in degree), but if a person forgives and makes reconciliation, his reward is due from God"* (42:40); *"And let them forgive, and let them forgo: don't you love that God should forgive you?"* (24:22).

An individual can ask God any time, any place, for forgiveness directly; he or she needs no intermediary or intercession, for every person, male or female, has a direct line to their Creator: whenever they cry for mercy and forgiveness, He responds and forgives. To go to a fellow mortal for confession, upon which he would say something to the effect of, "Go my child, you have been forgiven," has no place in Islam. Forgiveness is the domain of God alone, and no one else is ever in a position to play His role. As a matter of fact, there is no institution of clergy in Islam. Although there is theological scholarship, there is no priesthood.  With the hope that God's mercy is boundless, it is up to only Him to respond to us with justice (and He is the Absolutely Just) or with His mercy (and He is the Absolutely Merciful), and all our lives we pray He grants us His mercy rather than His justice.  Our repentance should be sincere and serious, and if it resides in the heart, it should show in the deeds.  It would be a contradiction if someone stole my wallet and refused to return it, repeating "Forgive me God" even a million times.  Justice should first be done when a third party is involved.

These doctrinal differences are neither trivial nor to be ignored, yet it would be foolish and counterproductive to fight one another or hate one another over them.  Debate over differences of belief should abide by the highest ethics of civilized debate:  *"And dispute you not with the People of the Book except in the most kindly manner—unless it be those of them who wronged—but say 'We believe in the Revelation which has come down to us and in that which came down to you; our God and your God is one, and it is to Him we submit (in Islam)'"* (29:46).

Notwithstanding the serious differences between the views of Christians and Muslims, Islam is very keen on expounding the common grounds and enjoying their spaciousness:  *"Say: O People of the Book. . . come to common terms as between us and you, that we worship none but God, that we associate no partners with Him, that we erect not from among ourselves Lords and Partners other than God: if they then turn back, then say 'Bear witness that we (at least) are Muslims (submitters to God's will)'"* (3:64).  Beyond that, relations should remain peaceful and friendly.

Having thus covered the religious (doctrinal) aspects, it is not out of place to briefly survey here the geopolitical history between Muslims and Christendom. At the time of the final prophet of Islam, the world was dominated by two major powers, the Persian Empire to the east and the Roman to the west. As the Persians were fire worshipers and the Romans were Christians, Muslims' sympathies naturally lay with the latter. A long military conflict raged between the two empires and the beginning of Islam witnessed a time of defeat for the Christians, but the Quran made the prophecy (which came true) that the tide would change: *"The Romans have been defeated, in a land close by, but they, (even) after this defeat of theirs, will soon be victorious within a few years. With God is the Command in the past and in the future. On that day shall the believers rejoice with (that) victory from God; He gives victory to whom He wills, and He is Exalted in Might, Most Merciful"* (30:2-5).

Years later, however, Islam prevailed in the Arabian peninsula and consolidated it into a state and an emerging political power, right at the flank of both giant empires. Both saw it as a serious threat and began to instigate hostilities against it, utilizing their client Arab tribes and, later, their colossal armed forces. The outcome of that inevitable military confrontation was almost miraculous, comparing the meagerness of the Islamic forces, both in number and in equipment, to the strength of their adversaries.

In the East the Persian dynasty came to an end and the people formerly under its domain, almost in totality, opted for Islam. In the West the authority of the Roman Empire was driven back, and in less than a century a pluralistic Islamic empire covered more than half of the known world at that time. This was the seat of the Islamic civilization that preserved the Greek heritage from annihilation by the Church and brought forth leaps of progress in various disciplines of knowledge such as medicine, chemistry, physics, astronomy, mathematics (algebra is an Arabic word and the science was invented by Muslims), music, philosophy, etcetera, apart from the religious sciences and Arabic literature and linguistics. People of all races and religions generously contributed to the development of this civilization.

Europe got its first shock out of the dark ages by witnessing this civilization without censorship (religious or otherwise) over the human mind. Arabic was the language of science; the earliest European universities employed Muslim professors and for many centuries used the books of Muslim authors. Europe learned about the Greek philosophers by translating their works from Arabic, and when the press was invented, most of its production was the translation of Arabic sources.

As the Muslim Empire weakened, Europe counterattacked. Amongst important historical developments were the Crusades in the East and the victory of Ferdinand and Isabella over Islamic Spain in the West. The latter gave birth to the Inquisition and the religious cleansing of Spain of the Muslims and Jews, and cleared the way for the discovery of the New World, the reign of the conquistadors and the establishment of a state-run slave trade.

The Crusades were an attempt to directly invade the Muslim heartland. At the time the justification was to free the Christian sacred places in Jerusalem from the Muslims, and for over two centuries the

Crusades evoked a religious furor that still lingers over the Western mind and shapes Western culture in some ways. This continues even though contemporary mainstream Christianity has condemned the Crusades and branded them as having been no more than colonialist-driven wars that donned the cloak of Christianity while committing such atrocities as to be an affront on Christianity itself.

The word "crusade" (both as a verb and noun) has settled in the language as a noble word, with deeply entrenched emotive overtones. We believe, along with many Christians, both clergy and laity, that Christendom should be re-educated on the Crusades in a spirit of soul-searching and self-appraisal, as has already been done with a large measure of success in regard to the Spanish Inquisition and the German Holocaust. A concerted effort to acknowledge the Crusades' true colors might be a crucial step in preparation for a New World Order, opening the gates of reconciliation between two blocks of humanity, each comprising one billion people, and perhaps helping to prevent similar evils from being camouflaged under a pseudo-religious aura, as in Bosnia and elsewhere in the world.

It is not my intention here to expound further on the Crusades with more than a few quotations of Christian authorship. Here is a crusader's report of the occupation of Jerusalem in the first Crusade, on July 15, 1099: "With drawn swords our people ran through the city; nor did they spare anyone, not even those pleading for mercy. If you had been there, your feet would have been stained up to the ankles with blood. What more shall I tell? Not one of them was allowed to live. They did not spare the women or children. The horses

waded in blood up to their knees, nay, up to the bridle.
It was a just and wonderful judgment of God."[9]

In 1202 the fourth Crusade took off from Venice and,
on the way, passed through Christian Constantinople,
where they rampaged the city and inflicted such atrocities that the Pope himself rebuked his own crusaders in a
message saying: "It was not against the Infidels but
against Christians that you drew your swords. It was not
Jerusalem that you captured, but Constantinople. It was
not heavenly riches upon which your minds were set but
earthly ones. Nothing has been sacred to you. You have
violated married women, widows, even nuns. You have
despoiled the very sanctuaries of God's Church, stolen
the sacred objects of altars, pillaged innumerable images
and relics of saints. It is hardly surprising that the Greek
Church sees in you the works of the Devil."[10] If this was
what the Crusaders did to Christian Constantinople, one
can imagine what they did to the "infidel" Muslims.

One of the significant milestones of modern times,
however, was the radical shift of the views of the Holy See
on Muslims, which should hopefully work as a catalyst for
better understanding between Muslims and Christians.
Whereas in 1095 Pope Urban II (also known as Urban
the Blessed), who was the first to call for the Crusades,
characterized Muslims as "Godless people, idolaters, enemies of Christ, dogs, chaff destined for eternal fire,"
etcetera, the encyclical *Nostra Aetate* of 1965 under Pope
Paul VI views Muslims in an entirely different light.

---

[9] Cohn, Norman. *The Pursuit of the Millennium.* Quoted in Bamber
Gascoigne, *The Christians,* by Bamber Gascoigne (London: Jonathan
Cape, London, 1977), 113.

[10] Gascoigne, Bamber. *The Christians.* London: Jonathan Cape, 1977,
119.

"Upon Muslims, too, the Church looks with esteem," the document says, and proceeds to expound that Muslims adore the One God, the God of Abraham, with whom the Islamic faith is happy to associate itself; worship, pray and give alms; revere Jesus and his virgin mother, and consider him a prophet and messenger of God.

Ever since the Crusades, the relation between Europe and the Muslim world has been distorted by the colonialist agenda of the European countries, and after World War I almost all Islamic countries were in the grips of European colonialism. A long struggle ensued that secured political independence, but colonialism merely took another from, neocolonialism, led by the United States of America, which does not depend on occupation armies but on economic leverage.

# Chapter Four

# THE ANATOMY OF ISLAM

The word *religion* in Western usage falls short of expressing the totality of Islam as a comprehensive system influencing all aspects of life, individual as well as communal. The total address of Islam to its followers is called the *Shari'ah*, and the division of the Shari'ah into the three compartments of worship, moral code and legal system is an arbitrary one, since these are closely interrelated and integrated. What is moral for the individual constitutes the norm for communal morality, and moralities do not exist in a legal vacuum. The inner self (conscience and intentions) and the outer self (deeds and observable behavior) should be in harmony and not conflict, and the system of worship prepares the individual to attain this reality of Islam. Anything less is fraudulent and counterfeit.

## A GENERAL OUTLINE OF THE SHARI'AH

### THE SOURCES OF THE SHARI'AH

The primary source of the Shari'ah is of course the Quran, the literal word of God. The Quran deals with a full spectrum of issues, ranging from the establish-

ment of the creed[11] to the definition of absolute moral
standards and codes of permissible and impermissible
behavior. It delineates the principles of worship and
lays down the framework of a comprehensive legal system relating to family law, economic rules, penal code,
social conduct, treaties, ethics of war and peace, pattern of government (and is considered the Islamic
forerunner of democracy), human rights, relations with
other nations and other religions, inheritance, taxation
(zakah), etcetera. It is true to say that there is hardly
an affair of life that lacks some reference in the Quran.

The Quran lays down a basic framework and
immutable principles concerning creed (*aqeeda*) and
worship (*ibadat*), whereas the domain of law governing human interaction (*mu'amalat*), barring a limited
number of exceptions, is regulated by flexible general
guidelines. The constants of the Shari'ah regarding
mu'amalat are therefore limited. This has contributed
immensely to the growth and evolution of the science
of jurisprudence (derivation of rulings), accommodat-
ing various schools of thought and amassing over the
centuries a wealth of opinions that have suited various
places and times and proved that the Shari'ah is neither static nor exhaustible.

The second source of the Shari'ah is the sunnah (tradition) of Prophet Muhammad in what he ordered, forbade, did or acknowledged in his capacity as prophet.
The sunnah at times explains the Quran, illustrates it,
details some of its generalities and complements it in
some areas. The sciences of sunnah, especially the process of the authentication of the sayings of the Prophet,

---

[11] See chapters one through three.

are perhaps the most exact branch in the science of history. The stringent guidelines followed by the compilers of the sunnah in their tracing of the chain of reporters and witnesses and, above all, their earnest efforts to ascertain that a reported sunnah was not in direct or indirect conflict with the Quran or with established fact and common sense, establish the sunnah as a science of precision.

The third source of the Shari'ah operates when an issue is not specifically settled by the Quran or the sunnah. Analogy is resorted to through a process of deductive reasoning that equates a new issue with one already decided by the Quran and/or sunnah. *Ijtihad* is the term indicating the utilization of available evidence (religious, scientific, statistical and social) to assay the best course to be taken, provided it does not conflict with the Quran or sunnah or with the goals of the Shari'ah, which will be presented shortly. The Shari'ah, therefore, is not a rigid set of rules to be copied and applied any time, any place. It allows for human ingenuity to address changeable situations through progressive legislation. During the evolution of the science of jurisprudence, juridical rules were established through the application of Islamic principles derived from the guidance of the Prophet and the Quran for new rulings in new situations. An example of this is the principle, *"Necessities overrule prohibitions."* For example, pork is unlawful to eat, but if it is the only food available to a traveler lost in the desert, it becomes permissible in amounts necessary for survival until lawful food becomes available. Examples of other rules include, "The lesser of two evils should be chosen when both together cannot be avoided," "Public interest takes precedence over individual interest," and "Harm is to

be removed." The overall rule, when there is no conflict with the Quran and sunnah, is "Wherever welfare
goes, there goes the statute of God."

## GOALS OF THE SHARI'AH

The supreme goal of the Shari'ah is the welfare of
the people, in this world and in the hereafter. Broadly
speaking, the needs of the community are classified
into dire necessities, ordinary necessities, and comple-
mentary needs (that make life more enjoyable), in this
order of significance. Topping the list is the first category, which comprises the widely known "Five Aims of
the Shari'ah," the objective of which is the preservation and protection of (1) life, (2) mind, (3) religion,
(4) ownership and possessions, and (5) procreation
and preservation of the species. Each of these is divided into further categories and branching subcategories
that include even seemingly minor details, and each is
serviced by appropriate moral and/or legal rulings.
Resisting all temptation to step into the deep waters of
this immense subject, we can glean the essential ideas
from each category to hopefully clarify the picture:

*Preservation and protection of life.* This includes
the right to life and the duty to protect it. It entails the
prohibition of killing and defines the permissible
exceptions, such as legitimate war or judiciary sen-
tence. To seek treatment when ill and to avoid ill
health by avoiding whatever leads to it are Islamic
duties, hence the dietary rules, encouragement of
physical fitness, and rules of cleanliness of person,
home, street, and environment. One of the impressive

teachings of Muhammad is that "God has not created an illness without creating a cure for it. . .some are already known and some are not," an impetus for continuing research. The principles of quarantine were established when Muhammad instructed, "If there is pestilence in a city, don't go in if you are out, or come out if you are already in."

Encouraging agriculture is commendable. Teachings of Prophet Muhammad include (1) If the Day of Judgment comes and you have in your hand a shoot to plant, hurry and plant it if you can; (2) Whoever cultivates a land will be rewarded for every soul eating from its harvest, even birds and animals, and even a thief who steals from it; (3) No trees should be cut or burnt as a means of warfare. Ecological awareness and respect for the environment are mandated. The water cycle is described in the Quran and its conservation and nonpollution was mandated by Muhammad. "No bird or animal is to be killed except for food" is one of his instructions, as is kindness to animals and refraining from overburdening them.

*Preservation and protection of mind.* The mind is the hallmark of a human being. It is our instrument by which we know good and evil and can explore God's creation and nature within and around us. Contemplation and reflection are religious duties, and the Quran condemns those who were given minds but do not use them. Freedom of thought and expression are basic human rights.

The pursuit of knowledge is not only a right but also a duty in Islam. The first word ever of the Quran is the command "*Read,*" and the Quran says, "*They are not equal, those who have knowledge and those who haven't, nor are light and darkness equal,"* and *"Of His servants the learned heed Him most."* Scientific research, in juridical jargon, is called "the revealing of God's tradition in His creation," and is a duty of those who are able to do it. Censorship over the mind is rejected, and no human being can claim authority over another in this respect. Not only should the mind be protected from censorship, but also from repression, fear, anxiety and stress. Anything that numbs or kills the mind is abhorrent; hence the consumption of alcohol and drugs are absolutely prohibited in Islam, not even in social proportions.

*Freedom of religion.* Many Islamic scholars give freedom of religion first place, but obviously without the integrity of life and mind, performance of religious duties is impossible. Freedom of religion and worship is a basic human right, and not for Muslims only. It is against Islam to coerce anyone to embrace it; the Quran says: *"There is no compulsion in religion"* (2:256). Houses of worship should be built, and any transgression against them is considered to be spreading of mischief in the land.[12] When Muslims are attacked on account of their religion, they have the right and duty of defense.

---

[12] The Quran says: "If God had not enabled people to defend themselves against one another, monasteries and churches and synagogues and mosques—in (all of) which God's name is abundantly extolled—would surely have been destroyed" (22:40).

*Protection of private ownership.* The right of ownership is inviolable and there is no objection or limit on the amassing of wealth, provided it is secured by lawful means. Unlawful means of collecting wealth are delineated by Islam, including usury, cheating and fraud, stealing, monopoly, etcetera. Rules of commercial dealings and exchanges are specified. The rights of capital are coupled with its duties, including taxation and contribution commensurate with the needs of society. The *zakah* tax is mandatory and equals roughly 2.5% of money hoarded over the span of one year, with other formulas for earnings from agriculture, animal husbandry, real estate and industry. The welfare of every individual is the joint responsibility of the whole community and no one can behave like an isolated island.

*Procreation and the preservation of the species.* Authentic marriage through a solemnized and documented marriage contract is the only legitimate way for a couple to pair off to form a family and beget children (the Shari'ah spells out the family ties that make the marriage of a couple impermissible). Purity of lineage (legitimate births by identified parents) and the right to know with certainty one's parents and one's progeny is a must. Breast-feeding is encouraged, optimally for two years.

Extramarital sex (including premarital sex) is sinful, and becomes a legally punishable offence if witnessed by four credible witnesses. Family planning (through natural or artificial means) is permitted, but not if it entails the killing of a life (i.e., abortion: the fetus has the right to life, inheritance and reception of a will or endowment). The pursuit of fertility and the treatment of infertility is allowed, but only as admissible in Shari'ah.

Western-style adoption is not allowed, but foster parentage or the sponsorship of needy children is encouraged as a charity, and those practices are devoid of the lie of claiming true family ties when they are, in reality, non-existent. Children are told the truth about their origins. Upon attaining adulthood, if a non-biological child reared within a family proposes to marry a biological child of the family, the proposal cannot be denied on the basis that they are brother and sister, since in reality they are not.

The mutual rights and duties of spouses, and between parents and children, are detailed. Family conduct and the rules of inheritance are specified. Sustaining the family is the obligation of the husband, whereas the financial contribution of the wife is her option. Women have the right to work (as compatible with the integrity of the family), and the absolute rights of independent individual ownership, inheritance, and education. Men and women are of equal human and spiritual worth, and the obligations (and prohibitions) of Islam apply to them equally.


## CHURCH AND STATE

Europe was wise in its decision to separate church and state. The near monopoly of the early church (versus the teachings of scriptures) over all aspects of life had no basis in the teachings of Jesus. Its power to obstruct freedom of thought and scientific progress is reflected in many well-known historical examples. Later, America followed a similar course for identical reasons, as well as to avoid one faith dominating the others in a religiously diverse society and thus interfering with freedom of religion. Many of the early immigrants to America were in fact fleeing the religious intolerance and persecution that afflicted European Christianity.

As I perceive it, the separation of church and state is consistent with the essential ideals of Christianity, for its primary purpose is to purify the human soul and ennoble the human character, not to pursue the organization of the state. Jesus' Kingdom, according to the New Testament, was not of this world. The New Testament reports that when asked whether it was lawful to pay tribute to the Roman Caesar, he looked at a coin with Caesar's inscription on it and said: *"Render unto Caesar what is Caesar's and unto God what is God's."* Muslims in the United States, like all other fair-minded people, appreciate the idea of pluralism that ensures the freedom of religion for all without bigotry or persecution, which as a matter of fact coincides with Islamic teachings.

Perhaps it is timely here to express a reservation felt by many Muslims, Christians and Jews, in America and the West, who feel that the principle of separation of church and state has been misused and manipulated to exclude God and the universal values of morality and decency received from Him from the daily life of people. The debate whether God is "dead" has been raging in the American media over the past three decades and has influenced the outlook of many. Many of those who believe that God is not dead have, in practice, ceased to acknowledge His authority to tell us what to do with our lives, as individuals and as a nation. Calls for moral behavior or against pornography, licentiousness, and other social ailments are often accused of violating the separation of church and state. The mottos "One nation under God" and "In God we trust" are becoming hollower by the day, and if things continue moving in the same direction, it may not be long before constitutional amendments to delete them altogether are actually implemented.

A universal reaction in the West of those who hear that Muslims in Islamic countries want to be ruled by the Islamic law is one of disapproval and dismay. Conditioned by the unfortunate European history that led to separation of church and state, they automatically abhor the idea and translate it as a regression to the dark ages when Europe toiled under the repressive authority of the church. This conclusion is not correct, because the two situations are not the same.

When we study the case of Islam, we find that the principle of separating church and state is obviously inapplicable. Whereas in Christianity there is no state, in Islam there is no church, which makes it impossible to project one situation on the other. Although there is scholarship, there is no clergy in Islam, nor is there an institution of priesthood. The fact that some graduates of Islamic studies in some Islamic countries don special garb has no religious significance and does not make them priests or elevate them in any way above other Muslims. No such garb was worn in the early days of Islam; it was a rather late development as society recognized special attire for special groups, such as the uniforms of the military and police and the white coat of the doctor. Religious knowledge and studies are open to all, and interpretation is not the monopoly or privilege of an elite group; scholastic specialization is appreciated and respected, but not sanctified. Nor is it part of Islam that only religious scholars should conduct the government, for obviously they may lack the technical expertise in the various divisions of the executive branches. Office should be held upon personal qualification and posts are open to both Muslim and non-Muslim citizens.

From even a cursory glance over the goals of the Shari'ah as given above, it is obvious that their implementation extends beyond the area of individual behavior, into the realm of government. The Shari'ah, the constitution, is the source of legislation and the foundation from which laws are to be derived. Although secularism in Christian societies is not incompatible with Christianity, the same cannot be said about Islam, for that would entail ignoring, inactivating or replacing many of the dictates of the Quran and sunnah, contradicting the basic creed of Islam. Appreciation of these facts should clarify the fact that what is agreeable to Christian societies might not be so to Muslim societies, though each promote the freedom of religion and the right to self-determination.

Neither Islamic nor Christian nations should impose their views on one another, but unfortunately this is not the case as the West, unilaterally, seems to be bent on preventing Muslims from self-rule in accordance with their own religion. It supports both secular dictatorships and dictatorships that falsely identify themselves as Islamic but are abysmal in the protection of human rights, the basic freedoms of men and women, and government by the people for the people, the hallmarks of real Islamic government. In fact there is virtually no state now that can be considered a representation of the true Islamic state. Whenever sound democratic process is about to lead to the victory of an Islamic party, a paradoxical and embarrassing alliance between the major democracies and the reigning dictatorships immediately intervenes to abort the attempt without considering giving it the chance to prove or disprove itself. Alas! The democracies are more keen on the status quo than they are on democracy itself.

One of the charges leveled against the demand of Islamic nations to be ruled by Islamic laws pertains to the status of Christian and Jewish minorities who are citizens of those countries. This objection is being played upon and blown up by both the media and politicians, although in reality it has no credence whatsoever. It is a little-known fact that the Islamic system, uniquely, leaves it to Christian and Jewish communities themselves to run their affairs of a legal nature in accordance with the guidelines of their own religions. Such issues, however, are few, and pertain to family issues (marriage, divorce, inheritance, and the like). Otherwise, with neither conflict with their scriptures nor alternative therein, the minorities will not be wronged and will stand equal with the majority before the law that the majority claims (out of religious conviction), in keeping with sound democratic principles.

We will not be completely honest, however, without voicing a few remarks and apprehensions about the question of implementing the Shari‘ah. In various instances it has been relegated to the realm of sloganism and emotionalism. Some overenthusiastic youth have transformed it into a confrontation with followers of other religions. The Shari‘ah, however, requires them to behave in a completely opposite way, aimed at dissipating fears, alleviating anxieties and exhibiting the ethics of good citizenship in a practical way, a task that mainstream Muslims and the great majority of Islamic movements are actively pursuing, although with hardly any coverage in the media or in professional political circles in the West.

Islamic political parties that decide on the democratic option are also in need of a word of advice here. Although they wage the electoral battle under the attractive banner of Islam, they should also present the electorate with the detailed programs they have prepared toward realizing the goals of the Shari‘ah. *Islam* is not a magic word that will solve the complex economic, social and political problems which burden their countries. Intense technical and specialized studies should be designed to work within the Shari‘ah toward appropriate solutions.

Those who opt for democracy are required by Islam to be honest in their declarations and must not commit the treachery of exploiting democratic rhetoric until they are in power, then abandoning it with the wind. The worst-case scenario is for an Islamic party to ride on democracy to power, fail to deliver promises, then refuse to acknowledge its failure, erroneously thinking that its failure will be ascribed to failure of Islam, and so, by either rigging or abolishing the following elections, denying the nation its right to remove them, and then, alas, becoming just another dictatorship! Islamic parties are yet to be tested on this, and it is unfair to prejudge them without trial.

The adversaries of these Islamic parties, who hold on to power against the will of their people, have been proven a failure, and the major democracies of the world should refuse to support them, morally or otherwise. If Islamic parties ever come to power, we advise them not to do the same, for it is not only Islamic laws that are needed, but above all, Islamic character and integrity as well. Some famous examples that claim, even boast, that they rule by the Shari'ah, are, in our opinion, lacking either in honesty or in knowledge about the Shari'ah, or both. Reducing the Shari'ah to a few selected items of its penal code without regard to its total context is a fraud. Meting out harsh punishment for petty crimes without any attempt at addressing the massive corruption in the ruling circles and their greedy exploitation of the nation's resources in total absence of accountability can never pass as Islamic.

In Islam the ruler is accountable to the nation and is considered its servant, not its master. It is against Islam to judge the commoners and the enfeebled while allowing the nobility to get away with violations. The Shari'ah must be implemented from beginning to end and not from end to beginning. To curb crime, Islam adopts a three-tiered approach: the cultivation of Islamic consciousness (through education and guidance), the prevention of problems that might lead to crime (social and economic), and finally, legal punishment—in that sequence. And then, the law knows no ceiling.


## DEMOCRACY

The question is quite often posed these days whether Islam is compatible with democracy. It is striking to note that those who say it is not are such a heterogeneous group, they hardly share anything else. Just as groups of Muslim intelligentsia at the turn of the century were so fascinated by the West that they called for the adoption of the good as well as the bad in the Western experience, the present time witnesses such disillusionment with the moral decline and the political injustices of the West that many reject, by way of reaction, all that is Western, including democracy. Secular dictators of Islamic countries, of course, abhor democracy by virtue of their being dictators and have a vested interest in presenting democracy to their Muslim masses as un-Islamic. Dictators who wear Islamic garb and claim to be Islamic also propagate the view that democracy is alien to the Islamic faith and have in their retinue and payroll religious scholars who are willing to play that Machiavellian role.

Traditional adversaries of Islam in the West, both in the media and political circles, also are relentlessly bent on featuring Islam as an anti-democratic religion that has no room for democratic values. Their aim, of course, is to further alienate Islam from the psyche of Western public opinion, making it both possible and palatable to demonize Muslims in a way that facilitates the acceptance of the harsh policies and unjust positions held by their governments against Muslims. They often raise the issue of the lack of democracy in the majority of Islamic countries. What they do not mention is that the only effective support of the dictators against the democratic aspiration of the peoples in the Middle East is provided by the Western democracies.

It is perhaps not feasible to compare the Islamic system that came into being early in the seventh century with the democratic institutions of the West, which began to evolve many centuries later. Nor are the Western democratic systems an exact replica of one another; they simply share the principles and ideology of democracy. The Quran (fourteen centuries ago) spelled out explicitly the principle of *shura*, which means that issues are to be decided by joint deliberation and consultation. The practical applications of this principle in the earliest days of Islam (the time of the Prophet and his immediate successors) qualify it to be considered the forerunner of democracy.

Only in his capacity as prophet was Muhammad to be obeyed without reserve, but outside the area of conveying and explaining religion as he received it from God, Muhammad himself made it clear that he was an ordinary human being who could not foretell the future or claim to have more knowledge than other people in their respective areas of expertise. On the eve of the Battle of Badr, the first and historically the most significant military encounter between Muslims and the Arab alliance of idolaters, the Prophet drew a military plan for deployment of his meager troops. When one of his followers then asked him, "Is this positioning revelation from God so that we have to abide by it without question, or is it an opinion of strategy and plan?" and Muhammad answered that it was indeed the latter, his companion suggested an alternate plan of deployment. The Prophet accepted his advice and adopted his plan; the outcome was a resounding victory.

Years later, the enemies dispatched a large army to attack the Muslims in Madinah. It was Muhammad's opinion to remain at Madinah and meet the enemy there, but discussions revealed that the majority preferred to march out and engage in battle with the enemy at Mount Uhud, well outside Madinah. Muhammad yielded to the majority opinion in compliance with the principle of shura. Muslims achieved an initial victory. At this, a battalion of archers positioned on the mountaintop thought the battle was over and, leaving their positions, they joined the chase, disobeying clear orders the Prophet had given them not to leave their positions no matter what happened. Khaled ibn al Waleed (a military genius who led a cavalry regiment of the enemy) noticed the weakness in the Muslim ranks, and circling back to the mountain's top, he attacked the Muslims from behind, taking them completely by surprise. This upset the balance and turned the tide against the Muslims; they had to retreat after incurring heavy losses. Although there was fault twice on the part of the Muslims, verses of the Quran were revealed shortly afterwards addressing Muhammad, *"And it was of the mercy of God that you dealt gently with them (your followers): had you been harsh-hearted, they would have broken away from you. So pardon them and ask (God) for their forgiveness and maintain shura with them"* (3:159). Shura is to pervade all walks of life at all levels, even in the seemingly small matters mentioned in the Quran, such as the Quranic commandment that the decision to wean a suckling infant should be taken by mutual shura (consultation) and consent of both parents.

The Prophet's death meant the conclusion of the prophethood, as there were to be no prophets after him, but he was to be succeeded by a head of state. The selection of a successor took place through an open debate, with more than one contender, until Abu

Bakr, the closest companion to the prophet, was chosen by consensus to be first caliph. On that occasion, established Islamic principle was reiterated and emphasized, most of all by Abu Bakr himself. We thus may sum up the significant rules governing the process of selection of a leader and his role in the Muslim community:

1. The post must be filled by the mandate of the people (Abu Bakr immediately proceeded to seek the opinion of others who were not in the meeting to make sure they concurred).

2. The appointment is conditional ("Obey me so long as I obey God," the caliph declared).

3. The right of the people to give the mandate is coupled with their right to withdraw it (Abu Bakr declared that if he acted against the law of God, then the people owed him no obedience).

4. The ruler is the nation's employee, hired by them to fulfil the duties of his office (seeing that Abu Bakr in his earliest few days pursued the management of his private business to make his living, the people imposed on him to accept a salary equal to the earnings of an average Muslim, neither rich nor poor, in lieu of working full time).

5. The head of state is no hostage to the elite, the nobility or special interest groups. He stated: "The weak amongst you is strong with me until I secure what is due to him, and the strong

amongst you is weak with me until I take from him what is due from him."

In short, it is the antithesis of what is practiced in the majority of Islamic countries nowadays. There is no doubt that if things had evolved in the direction prescribed by Islam, as the Islamic empire expanded and the Islamic civilization developed in maturity and sophistication, Muslims would have achieved a form of government that endorses the best in modern democracies while remaining free of their shortcomings.

Things went on in a very promising manner for some time. The second caliph, Omar, further alerted the nation of its duty to support him when right but to correct him if wrong, to which a man responded, "If you go astray we will correct you, even by our swords." The caliph's reply was, "You are no good if you don't say that, and we are no good if we don't accept that."

Unfortunately the trend was broken in one of the saddest, if not the saddest incident in Islamic history. Caliph Uthman had to face a rebellion accusing him of nepotism and was assassinated. Immediately succeeding Uthman in the caliphate, Caliph Ali was a cousin of the Prophet, his son-in-law, and a very beloved person to him. He also possessed outstanding personal merits, and when chosen for caliph, the notables and masses poured in to give allegiance. However, Muawiya, the governor of Syria (then part of the Islamic empire), refused to give the pledge and eventually marched towards Madinah at the head of a large army. His declared intention of marching against Madinah was to punish the assassins of Uthman, as he was related to the late caliph (both were from the Umayyad tribe); he demanded revenge rather than waiting for the results of lengthy due process of law. On the battlefield the victory was Ali's, but Muawiya was a resourceful man, and in his camp were some very shrewd men, so he secured a tricky arbitration. Some disgruntled people targeted both Muawiya and Ali for assassination, but succeeded only in killing Ali. The nation was shocked, but after negotiations, Hassan, Ali's son and successor, consented to yield authority to Muawiya to avoid further bloodshed and gave his allegiance.

A short while later Muawiya, well entrenched in authority, shocked the nation again by forcing from them a pledge to accept his son, Yazid, as successor after him, resorting to the technique of punishment and reward. Hussein, the second son of Ali, headed a revolution against Yazid (both Muawiya and Hassan had died by that time). The inhabitants of Iraq had promised Hussein their support, but under the trickery and brutality of the central government, they deserted him. Rather than flee or capitulate, Hussein and seventy loyal followers faced Yazid's army of several hundred thousand soldiers and bravely fought to their death at Karbala. This proved much later to have been the first nail in the coffin of the Umayyad dynasty, which reigned for some two centuries.

This event marked the birth of Shi'ism as a movement, comprised of hard-liners who called themselves the partisans of Ali (in Arabic, shi'a). The movement actually started as an expression of political dissidence, but one in which it was not possible to separate politics from religion, since striving for justice is a religious mandate. As time went on, Shi'ism took the form of an Islamic sect centered around the belief that eligibility to the caliphate should belong to Ali, then, consecutively, to his progeny (the eldest son in succession).

The Shi'ites acquired many secondary views as they broke into several sects, the major being the Twelver Shi'ites who believe that the twelfth of the successors (*imams*), who mysteriously disappeared as a child, will come back one day as the awaited Mahdi[13] and reign in justice. The Shi'ites constitute some ten percent of Muslims, and the remainder are traditionally called Sunnis. The Shi'ites tend to hold a grudge against the Sunnis for their early acquiescence to the alleged unjust authority, but all believe in the Quran and the prophethood of Muhammad. Every year the Shi'ites commemorate the Battle of Karbala and the martyrdom of Hussein, many of them slashing themselves mourning in remorse that their forebears deserted Hussein at the most critical moment of his struggle. It is a palpable fact that the Sunnis also have respectful and warm sympathies and sentiments towards Ali and his sons, Hassan and Hussein, and their households.

And now enough for history, even though we have tried to make it extremely brief, and back to the issue of democracy. The sad historical episode just related was the unfortunate precedent for transfer of power from hand to hand, not by the pledge of the nation but by sword and gold. The fallout from this unfortunate incident has persistently plagued subsequent Muslim history. Despotic rulers have always found learned

---

[13] Al-Mahdi: Lit. "the guided one," the righteous leader who is prophesied in some ahadith to come and lead the believers to victory before the Day of Judgment. Ed.

men eager to oblige and to rationalize, condoning their unjust rule, while others, who dared to speak out the unpalatable truth, paid with their lives or freedom. Things went well when the caliph was good and bad when he was bad, which was more often than not. In either case the authority of the people and their rights over the ruler were eroded. Islamic civilization, however, flourished because there have always been those who believe it is a religious duty to seek knowledge, excel in science and establish civilization. Government encouraged them in all these fields but suppressed efforts to talk or write about either the rights of the people versus the rulers or the restriction of their unbridled powers. Considering the genius of Islamic civilization in other walks of knowledge, we find that their writings on the constitutional rights of the people are powerful and marvelous, but scant.

To the Muslim brethren who convulse and contort against democracy, I would like to say that democracy has never been one of the ailments of the Muslim nation: its persistent affliction has been despotism and dictatorship. We would be blind if our history failed to reveal this fact to us. To those who accuse Islam of being intolerant to democracy, I say you are wrong, but there is a major difference between it and Islam. In a Western democracy, God can be vetoed or outvoted if His opponents can muster a majority vote. Under Islam the constitution is based on the Shari'ah, so any legislation that conflicts with it will be unconstitutional. Within that context, the democratic process takes its course one hundred percent.

The contemporary Islamic resurgence extends far beyond the widely publicized images of inflammatory extremism, violent expression or despotic secular and quasi-religious governments. A broad enlightened and quiet mainstream has discovered the realities of the religion and awakened to the lessons of history. It is not fueled by hollow sloganism against others, but by informed efforts toward just reformation. After all, Islamic scholars have long decreed that a non-Islamic state which observes justice is better than an Islamic state riddled with tyranny and injustice.

## THE INNER SELF

### THE FIVE PILLARS OF ISLAM

Chapters one and two dealt with the articles of faith, defined in the words of Prophet Muhammad: "That you believe in God, His angels, His Books, His messengers, the Last Day, and fate or pre-destination (belief in predestination does not negate the concept of free will, but refers to that which one has no control over, whether good or bad)." In our presentation we did not present these articles as a 'dogma' that is to be accepted blindly, but tried to explain them logically. This is in keeping with the way of the Quran, which challenges the human mind to think, pointing to signs and posing questions to contemplate, not to impose belief but to convince.

The creed of Islam (that there is only One God) along with its articles of faith, is similar to that of the other Abrahamic religions, Christianity and Judaism. Indeed Islam describes the previous messengers of

God and their followers as Muslims following Islam, the literal meaning of *Islam* being submission to the will of God. Having presented in this chapter a general map of the Islamic religion and its Shari'ah, we'll discuss in this section an aspect that is more specific to Islam, which is its system of worship. Worship is central to Islam since it focuses on the individual Muslim in order that the Islamic collectivity be made of healthy units, or in other words, that the building be made of sound blocks.

Mandatory worship in Islam comprises five areas, as described by Prophet Muhammad: "Islam is built on five pillars: the declaration (bearing witness) that there is no god but God (Allah) and that Muhammad is His messenger, the establishment of prayers, the payment of the zakah (alms-tax), the observation of the fast of Ramadan, and the hajj (pilgrimage) if one is capable of it." On another occasion, when the Prophet was asked to give a definition of Islam, he named these five pillars. Needless to say, buildings do not consist of pillars, rather, pillars exist to support whole buildings. Those who reduce Islam to the area of ritual worship naturally lack an understanding of the comprehensive and total nature of Islam and of the purpose that these acts of worship are meant to serve in molding the character of the worshipper.

The "five pillars of Islam" are the minimum requirement of worship; any lawful act performed with the intention of pleasing God is considered to be worship of Him, and charitable pursuits are open without limit, down to the smallest detail of meeting people with a smiling face or removing harmful objects from the street, both deeds enjoined on believers by Prophet

Muhammad. Practically all of one's actions can become, upon one's intention, legitimate acts of worship. We will now briefly discuss each of these pillars.

*The declaration (shahadah).* The simple statement 'I bear witness there is no god but Allah and that Muhammad is His messenger' is the password into Islam. Uttering it with sincerity before two witnesses is all the formality required from new converts to Islam. The *shahadah* is also included in the call to prayer (the *adhan*) and repeated during all prayers. And yet it is more than a verbal formality, for when you declare that you take God as your God, it means that you take Him as the shaper and guider of your life, refusing to be swayed by other influences, be they people, things, moods or desires. The person who professes that Muhammad is God's messenger in fact pledges to abide by the instructions and teachings of Muhammad and to acknowledge their divine source. In Islamic jurisprudence and in literature over the ages, lengthy works have been written on the far-reaching implications of declaring *"There is no god but God, and Muhammad is His messenger."*

*Prayer (salah).* The ritual prayer of Islam is a distinct entity, somewhat different from prayer in its wider sense, that is, communicating your feelings to God at any time in any place and asking for His guidance, help and forgiveness, a practice that is ordained by the Quran and commendable in other religions. Ritual Islamic prayer takes a special form and content, in which both body and soul are harmoniously involved. It is performed five times a day: at early morning, early afternoon, late afternoon, after sunset and after dark.

The prayers may be performed at any clean place (home, mosque, park, the workplace, etcetera) by an individual or by a group, Muslim men and/or women, with one of the men leading the prayers as an *imam* (leader). The five prayers each take only a few minutes to perform. Only the noon prayer on Friday is mandated to be a collective (group) prayer, which is held at the mosque and preceded by a sermon (*khutba*). The imam (prayer leader) is not a priest, nor does the same person have to lead each prayer, but considerations of scholarship and knowledge of the Quran and the religion are exercised in choosing him (business-people, blue-collar workers, doctors, teachers, and others, as well as religious scholars, commonly bear this responsibility).

In order to perform the prayer one has to be clean, having performed an ablution (*wudu*) entailing cleaning by water of the mouth, nostrils, face, forearms to the elbows, and feet, and wiping the head and ears with wet hands. An ablution may take one through several prayers but must be repeated if one falls asleep or passes urine, stools, or flatus. Sexual intercourse necessitates a full bath. Women are exempted from the ritual prayers during their menstrual (and puerperal) flow, and at its cessation, a bath is necessary, as it is for men after ejaculation. However, anyone may pray to God at any time, in personal supplication, with or without wudu.

Each prayer is practically an audience with God. Facing in the direction of the Kaaba (the first mosque ever, built by patriarch Abraham and his son Ishmael for the worship of the One God, at the site which long later became the city of Makkah in Arabia). Only around the Kaaba mosque in Makkah do Muslims stand in concentric circles for their prayers (quite an impressive scene). All the world over they pray standing in straight lines, leaving no gaps, and facing Makkah. Women usually occupy the back lines, not necessarily a requirement of religion but an aesthetic preference, since women would feel uncomfortable with men behind them during the movements of bowing and prostration.

The prayer is opened by reciting the words *Allahu Akbar*, i.e., God is Greater (than all else), with which the worshipper practically turns his or her back to all the universe and addresses God. One necessary component of each of the prayers is the Opening Chapter of the Quran, which reads: *"Praise be to Allah, Lord of the worlds. The Compassionate, the Merciful, Master of the Day of Judgment. You alone do we worship and You alone we ask for help. Guide us to the straight path, the path of those on whom You have bestowed Your grace, those who are not deserving of Your wrath, and who go not astray"* (1:1-7). The rest of the prayer consists of reciting additional portions of the Quran, and of bowing down and prostrating oneself (to God), interjecting *"Glory to my Lord the Greatest," "Glory to my Lord the Highest," "Allah listens to those who thank Him,"* and what fills one's heart by way of supplication. The prayer is concluded in the sitting position by reiterating the affirmation of the faith (the shahadah), and seeking God's peace and blessings on prophets Muhammad and Abraham and their families and followers.

Prayer, both obligatory and spontaneous, is an immense spiritual treasure to be tapped. It inspires peace, purity and tranquility, and instills a continuous awareness of and feeling of closeness to God. It amazingly reduces the hustle-and-bustle of life to tame proportions. By their spacing of five times a day, including at the day's beginning, prayers tend to help worshippers maintain a therapeutic level of well-being and practically leave no room in their consciousness for mischievous thought or deed.

*The alms tax (zakah)*. Spending money in charity is highly commendable, and Muslims are encouraged to spend as much as they can; the sky is the limit. But zakah, the third pillar of Islam, is different because it is obligatory, not voluntary, and it is given in a calculated amount. In general terms, what remains over and above the meeting of one's needs and expenses and is hoarded for the full span of one year must be purified by zakah, in the amount of two and one-half percent. Idle money is, in effect, thereby penalized by complete depletion over a period of about forty years, which is an incentive to put money to work and thus serve the public interest. In addition to money, other forms of gain and profit have their respective formulas, including the proceeds from industry, agriculture and animal husbandry, real estate, etcetera, as is thoroughly detailed in specialized references.

Zakah is the *right* of the poor in the wealth of the rich and is neither optional charity nor philanthropy. In an Islamic state it is collected by the government and is a primary source of budget, to be complemented as necessary by other legislated taxation. It may be given to voluntary Islamic institutions, which are then responsible for its just distribution, or directly to the needy in locations where Islamic law does not operate (as in the case of Muslims living as minorities all over the world or under secular rule). Needy non-Muslims may be included as beneficiaries.

Zakah represents the unbreakable bond between members of the community, whom Prophet Muhammad described as "like the organs of the body, if one suffers then all others rally in response." Literally, the word *zakah* means "purification" in Arabic, meaning that one purifies one's money by giving the needy their just portion out of it. As Muslims pay the zakah, they have the genuine feeling that it is an investment and not a debit.

*Fasting in Ramadan (sawm).* The month of *Ramadan* is part of the Islamic lunar calendar, and since it is eleven days shorter than the Gregorian calendar, Ramadan comes eleven days earlier each year, which allows fasting in various seasons and weathers throughout one's lifetime. From dawn to sunset during each day of Ramadan, Muslims go without any food or drink (not even water). Sex also is banned during the daytime, and to preserve one's fast, one should not exihibit anger or any other misbehavior.

Ramadan is not a month of starvation, since nutrition and hydration are ensured at night. It is recommended, however, that one should exercise moderation while taking evening and pre-dawn meals. Those who are ill, children, nursing mothers, and the elderly are exempt from fasting.

As one conquers the pull of daily habits and endures hunger and thirst, Ramadan furnishes a first class drill in self-restraint and willpower (and what would humanity be if the faculty of self restraint were lost?). Fasting

becomes a very enriching experience as one transcends
the needs of our material component and cherishes the
spiritual. The month is a period of spiritual renewal and
revitalization, and is almost like charging one's batteries
for the rest of the year. Intensified worship and charity
are a feature of this month. At its conclusion Muslims
celebrate one of their two *eids* (religious feasts)—the
other one being at the conclusion of the pilgrimage season—by a special collective morning prayer and by fes-
tive gatherings with family and friends.

*The pilgrimage (hajj).* Islam relates so profoundly
to the monotheistic mission of Abraham that its fifth
pillar (hajj) is none but a formal commemoration of the
patriarch Abraham's obedience to God. Prophet
Abraham (peace be upon him) consistently obeyed
God throughout the many trials he endured in life. In
one test, God ordered him to take his wife, Hagar, and
his only son at the time, Ishmael, to the seemingly des-
olate region of southwestern Arabia. Putting his trust
in God for their welfare, Abraham left his wife and
child at the site of the future city of Makkah. Soon
after his departure, when their provisions were nearly
depleted and Ishmael's mother had to go through the
ordeal of searching for water in panic and near despair,
the Well of Zam-Zam unexpectedly and miraculously
erupted. Abraham, who periodically visited them, was
later ordained by God to build, with the assistance of
Ishmael, the first mosque for the worship of God and to
call the believers to visit or make pilgrimage (hajj) to
that mosque in worship. The most strenuous test for
Abraham was no doubt the divine command to slay his
own son, which he, with the encouragement of the son

himself to carry out the command of God, obeyed. God, having tested the sincerity and faith of Abraham, spared the boy and ransomed him with a ram.

The pilgrimage therefore started with Abraham and Ishmael and has continued unbroken ever since. Unfortunately, however, people after many generations slipped into paganism and transformed the house of God's worship into a house for idols. Each tribe of the pagan Arabs took an idol, gave it a name, and placed it in the Kaaba. The pilgrimage season continued to be observed, but instead of being a time to worship God, it became a season of merriment and festivity, drinking and vice, and new rituals were improvised, such as encircling the Kaaba in the nude while clapping, singing and whistling. The adulterated institution of pilgrimage was a great financial bonanza for the people of Makkah, whose economy was based on the season and on two annual caravan journeys for transit trade between the East (Africa and Asia) and West (Syria and beyond to the Byzantine Empire). A pseudo-clergy arose to speak on behalf of the gods and accept offerings and pledges made to them.

For thousands of years this state of affairs continued on the part of this (Ishmael's) side of the seed of Abraham. Then, out of the distant progeny of Ishmael, from the powerful tribe of Quraish, Muhammad was born in the year 570 C.E. His father died before he was born, and his mother in his early childhood. Muhammad was raised by his grandfather, and when the latter died, by one of his uncles. As he grew up he became a focus of the respect and admiration of all his community, and at quite an early age he was nicknamed "the honest." At the age of twenty-five he married a wealthy widow, Khadija, for whom he had worked as caravan trade manager and who valued his character. She was fifteen years his elder, but they lived happily in a monogamous marriage for the next twenty-eight years until she died.

Muhammad never shared with his people their worship of idols or the various wrongs that were the very life of the pre-Islamic (*jahiliyya*, i.e., days of ignorance) Arabs. He habitually visited a cave at the top of a mountain near Makkah to reflect and meditate, and during one of those visits, the Angel Gabriel appeared to him, conveyed the divine assignment of prophethood, and gave him the first revelation ever from the Quran, which states: *"Read! In the name of thy Lord who created. . .created man out of a clinging clot. Read; and thy Lord is the Most Bountiful, He (it is) who taught with (the use of) the pen, taught man what man knew not"* (96:1-5). The month was Ramadan, and the night was the Night of Power (in Arabic, *layl la-tul qadr*). Muhammad was over-awed, and hurried home shivering and trembling, where his wife comforted and calmed him, saying: "By Him who dominates Khadija's soul, I pray that you will be the prophet of this nation. You are kind to your kin, generous to the guest, helpful to the needy and truthful in your speech; God will not let you down."

The angel visited again and again, throughout Muhammad's prophethood. Although his appointed mission brought the truth and marked the turning of his people back to the pure monotheism of Abraham, nothing could be more threatening to the alliance between the rich and powerful and the idolatrous clergy of Makkah, whose very existence depended on the status quo. For thirteen years Muhammad and his followers were persecuted, until they emigrated to their base in Madinah and were permitted (by the Quran) to defend themselves and strengthen their position. Eventually Muhammad's army conquered Makkah, declaring general amnesty for those who had fought against the Muslims and Islam. They destroyed the idols, purifying the Kaaba of Abraham from paganism and restoring the religion to its pure source. Pilgrimage went on at its specified season, and the fifth pillar of Islam was mandated for every Muslim man and woman, once in a lifetime, for those who are physically capable of it and financially able to afford it.

Despite the well-known facts outlined above in this rather lengthy explanation, there are yet "experts" and "scholars" who describe the hajj (pilgrimage) simply as "a pagan ritual incorporated by Islam." Isn't this sufficient cause for the Muslim to feel put out?

The pilgrimage season comes with the twelfth month of the lunar calendar, which is called the month of the hajj (*Dhul Hijja*), already known when Islam came, since it was an Abrahamic event. During hajj, women wear ordinary clothes that cover the whole body, except the face and hands. Men must wear two pieces of white unsewn cloth, without any other clothing except, perhaps, sandals and a (pocketed) belt. This is the universal dress and the pilgrims all look alike, without any class distinctions, and they mingle together in full brotherhood and with prompt eagerness to offer help to one another whenever possible, overlooking and transcending all differences in color, language, race, ethnicity, degree of education, etcetera. During hajj only the goodness of humanity and the purity of the belief that humanity is *one* family worshipping *one God* is evident. There is no segregation, and families and other groups try to stick together so none becomes lost amongst the millions.

Hajj rituals include worship at the Mosque of Abraham and circumambulation of the Kaaba; several to-and-fro walks between the hills of Safa and Marwah, where prophet Ishmael's mother, Hagar, frantically ran in search of water for her son; the assembly around Mount Arafat in prayer and supplication; and stopping at the three sites (where the devil tried to tempt Abraham against slaying his son) and throwing pebbles at the pillars placed there, symbolic of conquering temptation by the devil. The highlight of hajj is the collective prayer and sermon on the *Eid ul-Adha* (feast of sacrifice), followed by sacrificial slaughter of a ram (donated to the poor, but part goes to family and friends), following the tradition of Abraham. Muslims who are not in attendance at the pilgrimage celebrate the eid by collective prayer (including a sermon) and the sacrificial offering of a sheep.

The eid feast is a happy occasion to rejoice in. In view of the large number of animals sacrificed near Makkah at the hajj, which cannot possibly be consumed there and then, the Saudi Arabian authorities have established a meat packaging plant (upon securing the necessary fatwa or religious opinion) in order to preserve and can the meat for leisurely shipment to the poor and needy in the Islamic world. Their efforts to accommodate, manage, and facilitate the mass movements of the pilgrims (at least two million) within a tight schedule of time and space are to be commended.

## ISLAMIC MORALITY

Islamic morality is comparable to Christian morality and Jewish morality in their pure form as prescribed by the Torah and the Injil and devoid of the latter-day revisionism of groups that have played havoc with the Abrahamic moral heritage and changed the moral code in such a way that made the immoralities of yesterday look like the moralities of today. These immoralities have been coated with new innocuous and euphemistic terms, such as "love," "gay," "relationship," "boy/girlfriend," "lover," etcetera, by those who hoped that nice names might camouflage (or help promote) the sins of old.

Instead of discussing individual issues, we thought it a better use of this section to introduce the reader directly to the source of Islamic morality by referring to a number of quotations from the Quran and the *hadith* (sayings) of the prophet Muhammad. It is information that the Western reader is particularly unaware of and is separated from by layers upon layers of negative indoctrination by so-called experts and specialists. So many times have we read or heard on radio and television that the Quran orders Muslims to lie, cheat, or kill non-Muslims, or that Muhammad was a ruthless villain, drunk with his own ambitions and fondness for lust and sensuality. We try to refute falsehoods and sometimes succeed in getting an answer published or even in getting an apology, but the flow of disinformation continues. Yet, at our varied initiatives, more and more people are coming to know the truth about Islam, and once a minimal critical mass of individuals are able to differentiate the false from the true, it will be the end of a campaign of malevolence and stereotyping upon which many have made their career.

Islamic morality is not merely a list of do's and don'ts. It aims at building a personality that understands and accepts the role of man as God's vicegerent on earth, so that a person is willing to manage the nature within and the nature outside of himself or herself in harmony with the Owner's (God's) manual. We give below some excerpts, with no other order than that in which they came to memory.

## A TASTE OF THE QURAN

1. *And the servants of (Allah) the Most Gracious are those who walk on the earth in humility, and when the ignorant address them they say, "Peace!" And those who spend the night in adoration of their Lord, prostrate and standing. Those who say "Our Lord! Avert from us the wrath of Hell," for its wrath is indeed an affliction grievous. Evil indeed is it as an abode and as a place to rest in. Those who, when they spend are not extravagant and not miserly, but hold a just (balance) in between those (extremes). Those who invoke not with God any other deity, nor slay such life as God has made sacred except for just cause; nor commit adultery, and any that does this (not only) meets punishment, (but) the chastisement on the Day of Judgment will be doubled to him, and he will dwell therein in ignominy: unless he repents, believes and works righteous deeds, for God will change the evil of such persons into good, and God is Oft-*

*Forgiving, Oft-Merciful. And whoever repents and does good has truly turned to God in repentance. Those who give no false witness, and if they pass by futility, they pass by it with honorable avoidance. Those who, when they are admonished with the signs of their Lord, droop not down at them as if they were deaf and blind. And those who pray: "Our Lord, grant unto us spouses and offspring who will be the comfort of our eyes, and give us (the grace) to lead the righteous." (25:63-74)*

2. *Be quick in the race for forgiveness and for a garden whose width is that (of the whole) of heavens and earth, prepared for the righteous: Those who spend (on others) freely, whether in prosperity or in adversity; who restrain anger and pardon all people, for God loves those who do good. And those who, having done an act of indecency, or wronged their own souls, remember God and ask for forgiveness for their sins—and who can forgive sins except God?—and are never obstinate in persisting knowingly in that (wrong) they have done. For such, the reward is forgiveness from their Lord and gardens with rivers flowing underneath: an eternal dwelling, how excellent a recompense for those who work (and strive). (3:133-136)*

3. *Behold, Luqman said to his son admonishing him: "O my son! Join not in worship (others) with Allah (God): for false worship is indeed the highest wrong-doing." And We have enjoined on*

*man (to be good) to his parents. In travail upon travail did his mother bear him, and in years twain was his weaning. Hence (O man): Show gratitude to Me and to your parents; to Me is the final goal. But if they strive to make you join in worship with Me things of which your mind cannot accept, obey them not, yet bear them company in this life with kindness, and follow the ways of those who turn to Me; in the end the return of you all is to Me and I will tell you all that you did. "O my son (said Luqman), if there be but the weight of a mustard seed and it were (hidden) in a rock, or (anywhere) in the heavens or on earth, God will bring it forth, for God is Subtle and Aware. O my son! establish the prayer, enjoin what is just and forbid what is wrong; and bear with patient constancy whatever betides you, for this is firmness (of purpose) in the conduct (of affairs). And swell not your cheek (for pride) at people, nor walk in insolence through the earth, for God loves not arrogant boasters. And be moderate in your pace, and tame your voice, for the harshest of sounds without doubt is the braying of the ass." (31:13-19)*

4. *Let not those among you who are endued with grace and amplitude of means resolve by oath against helping their kinsmen (even who had done them injustice), those in want and who have left their homes in the cause of God. Let them forgive and overlook: do you not wish that God should forgive you? For God is Oft-Forgiving, Most-Merciful. Those who slander chaste, unsus-*

*pecting and believing women are cursed in this life, and in the hereafter for them is a grievous chastisement.* (24:22-23)

5. *It is not righteousness that you turn your faces towards East or West, but it is righteousness to believe in God and the Last Day and the angels and the Book and the messengers; to spend of your substance, out of love for Him, for your kin, for orphans, for the needy, for the wayfarer, for those who ask, and for the freeing of slaves; to be steadfast in prayer and give zakah; to fulfil the contracts which you have made; and to be firm and patient in suffering, adversity and times of panic. Such are the people of truth, the God-fearing.* (2:177)

6. *Verily, for all men and women who have submitted (to the will of God), for believing men and women, for devout men and women, for truthful men and women, for truly patient and constant men and women, for humble men and women, for charitable men and women, for men and women who fast, for men and women who guard their chastity, and for men and women who engage much in the remembrance of God: for them has God forgiveness and great reward.* (33:35)

7. *God commands justice, the doing of good and giving to kith and kin, and He forbids indecencies, evil and offence; He instructs you that you may receive admonition. Fulfil the covenant of God when you have entered into it, and break not your oaths after you have confirmed them:*

*indeed you have made God your surety, for God knows all that you do.* (16:90-91)

8. *Your Lord has decreed that you worship none but Him and that you be kind to parents. Whether one or both of them attain old age in your life, say not to them a word of contempt, nor repel them: but address them in terms of honor. And lower to them the wing of humility out of compassion, and say "My Lord, bestow on them your mercy even as they cherished me in childhood."* (17:23-24)

9. *It may be that God will establish friendship between you and those whom you (now) hold as enemies, for God has power (over all things) and God is Oft-Forgiving, Most-Merciful. God forbids you not with regard to those who do not fight you for your religion nor drive you out of your homes, from dealing kindly and justly with them: for God loves those who are just.* (60:7-8)

10. *O you who believe! Stand out firmly for God as witnesses to fair dealing, and let not the hatred of others make you swerve to wrong and depart from justice. Be just, that is closeness to piety; and fear God, for God is well acquainted with all that you do.* (5:8)

11. *O you who believe: Let not some men among you deride others; it may be that the latter are better than they (are). Nor let some women (deride) other women who may be better than*

*they are. Nor defame nor be sarcastic to each other, nor call each other by (offensive) nicknames: bad is a name connoting wickedness (to be used of one) after he has believed, and those who do not desist are indeed doing wrong. O you who believe! avoid much suspicion, for suspicion in some cases is a sin. And do not spy on each other. Nor backbite one another: would any of you like to eat the flesh of his dead brother? You abhor that (so abhor the other)! And fear God, for God is acceptor of repentance, Most Merciful. (49:11-12)*

12. *But if the enemy inclines towards peace, do (you) also incline towards peace, and trust in God, for He is the One that hears and knows (all things). (8:61)*

13. *Nor can goodness and evil be equal; repel (evil) with what is better: then will he between whom and you was enmity become as it were an intimate friend. (41:34)*

14. *Have you seen him who gives the lie to the religion? Such is the one who repulses the orphan and does not prompt the feeding of the indigent. So woe to those who pray (but) are absent-minded about their prayers, those who want (but) to be seen, but refuse (even) small kindnesses. (107:1-7)*

15. *Woe to those who deal in fraud, those who, when they have to receive by measure from others, exact full measure, but when they have to give by*

*measure or weight to others, give less than due. Do they not think that they will be raised up on a mighty day, a day when (all) mankind will stand before the Lord of the Worlds?* (83:1-6)

## THE PROPHET SPOKE

1. *None of you (truly) believes until he wishes for his brother what he wishes for himself.*

2. *Whosoever of you sees an evil action, let him change it with his hand; and if he is not able to do so, then with his tongue; and if he is not able to do so, then with his heart—and this is the weakest of faith.*

3. *Your Lord (God) said: "O son of Adam, so long as you call upon Me and ask of Me, I shall forgive you for what you have done, and I shall not mind. O son of Adam, were your sins to reach the clouds of the sky and were you then to ask forgiveness of Me, I would forgive you. O son of Adam, were you to come to Me with an earthful of sins and were you then to face Me (in sincere repentance) ascribing no partners to Me, I would bring you an earthful of forgiveness."*

4. *God does not look at your bodies and figures, but looks at your hearts and your deeds.*

5. *People are equal like the teeth of a comb. You are all from Adam: and Adam is from dust. There is no superiority of white over black, nor of Arab over non-Arab, except by piety.*

6. *The strong person is not the one who is good at wrestling. The strong person is the one who controls himself when angry.*

7. A young man asked the Prophet: "'Who of all people is most worthy of my kindness?" The Prophet answered, *"Your mother."* The man asked: "Then who (is next)?" The Prophet answered, *"Your mother."* The man asked again "Then who?" and the Prophet answered, *"Your mother."* The man asked yet again "Then who?" And then the Prophet answered, *"Your father."*

8. *The best of you are those who are most kind to their wives. And I am the best amongst you.*

9. The Prophet was asked: "Could a believer ever be a coward?" and he answered *"Maybe."* "Could a believer be miserly?" the Prophet was asked, and he answered *"Maybe."* But when asked "Could a believer be a liar?" the Prophet answered *"No. Never!"*

10. *On a hot summer day, a man found a thirsty dog at the edge of a well, unable to reach the water. He said to himself,* "This dog must be suffering from thirst as I am now." *The man went into the well, filled his shoe with water and offered it to the dog to drink. God was pleased with him, and granted him forgiveness of his sins.*

11. *The signs of the hypocrite are three: when he speaks, he lies; when he promises, he breaks (the promise); and when he is entrusted, he betrays the trust.*

12. *Your Lord (God) says: "When My servant comes close to Me as much as the span of a hand, I come to him as much as a forearm; and when he comes to Me as far as a forearm, I come to him as far as outspread arms; and when he comes to Me walking, I come to him running."*

13. *Angel Gabriel advised me continuously to take care of my neighbor until I thought that God would make him an inheritor.*

14. *When the Day of Judgment takes place, a call will be heard saying: "Where are those who used to forgive other people? Come forth toward your Lord and receive your rewards. It is for every forgiver to be admitted to heaven."*

15. *O God! I seek refuge in You from wrong and sorrow. I seek refuge in You from cowardliness and stinginess. And I seek refuge in You from debt and from being overpowered by people.*

16. *When an abomination settles among a people and they further publicize and promote it, then surely God will cause in them illnesses that were unknown to their forebears.*

17. *Liquor (alcoholic drinks) is the mother of evils.*

18. *How amazing the affairs of the believer are, because there is good for him in all affairs. If he receives a good thing he is grateful (to God) and this is good for him, while if he is struck with adversity, he is patient and it is good for him.*

19. *When a child of Adam dies, he is completely cut off (from this world) in the hereafter except for three things (whose blessings shall reach him): a perpetual charity, useful knowledge that others continue to gain from, and a pious child praying for him.*

20. *The most hateful to God of the things that He has made lawful is divorce. The believer should (if at all possible) not abandon his believing wife: if she has some aspects that he does not like, she surely has also other aspects that he likes.*

21. *Seven people are sheltered by the shade of God on the Day of Judgment, when there is no shade but His: a just leader, a youth raised in the obedience of God, a man whose heart is devoted to mosques, two brothers (or sisters) whose fraternity is for God, a person who remembered God in his privacy and tears flooded his eyes, a young man whom a woman of beauty attempted to seduce but he replied "I fear God," and a man who gave to charity in silence so that his left hand did not know what his right had spent.*

22. *Whoever has eaten raw onion and garlic should keep away from the congregational prayer at the*

*mosque (lest he should cause offense to others because of its strong smell).*

23. *The example of those who (faithfully) abide by God's commandments and those who do not is like a group of travelers who shared a ship, some on the upper deck and some below. When the latter needed water, they had to go up to bring it, so they said, "Let us make a hole in our part of the ship (to get water) directly." But if those on the upper deck allowed them to do what they had suggested, all of them would be destroyed, while if they prevented them from doing so, all of them would be safe.*

24. *The upper hand (i.e. the one that gives) is better than the lower hand (that takes).*

25.  The Prophet said, *"Support your brother whether right or wrong."* Thereupon he was asked:  "We (understand) supporting him if he is right, but how could we support him if he was wrong?" The Prophet answered:  *"By preventing him from doing wrong:  for this is his real (help) support."*

26. *Nations before you met their destruction because when the sons of nobility stole, they acquitted them, but when the weak stole, they punished them.*

27. *Work for this world as if you are to live forever, and work for your hereafter as if you are to die tomorrow.*

28. Some poor Muslims complained to the Prophet: "The affluent have made off with (all) the rewards: they pray as we pray, fast as we fast, and they give away in charity from their money (and this we can't match)." The Prophet said: *"Has not God made things for you to give away in charity? Every praise to God of His perfection is a charity. Every thankfulness to God is a charity. Every utterance that there is no God but God is a charity. To enjoin good and forbid evil is charity. And each time you go to your wife is a charity."* They said: "One satisfies his sexual desire and is rewarded for it?" He said *"Do you (not) think that if he were to satisfy his desire unlawfully he would be sinning? Likewise, if he satisfies his desire lawfully, he will have a reward for doing so."*

29. The Prophet was asked about the best (in heeding God). He said: *"To heed Him as if you see Him, for even though you don't see Him, He sees you."*

30. *Be mindful of God, you will find Him before you. Get to know God in prosperity and He will know you in adversity. Know that what has passed you by could not have befallen you, and that what has befallen you could not have passed you by, and know that victory comes with patience, relief with affliction, and ease with hardship.*

# Chapter Five

# LIVE ISSUES

As a comprehensive religion dealing with the whole of life and not confined to matters of worship or the house of worship, Islam shares the concerns of society at large, of which Muslims are a part. Naturally, Muslims wish to share their values with others in an attempt to jointly explore solutions and common ground in the resolution of these problems.

In this chapter we will present the Islamic view of some contemporary issues. The topics were selected only as specimen cases by which to examine and demonstrate the relevance of the Islamic perspective to our everyday life, moving away from the area of theory and abstract thought.

The subjects discussed in the following pages are (1) the New World Order, (2) jihad, (3) family and the sexual revolution, and (4) biomedical ethics, including (a) reproductive issues, (b) organ donation and transplantation, (c) definition of death, (d) euthanasia, and (f) genetic engineering.

# THE NEW WORLD ORDER

The declaration of a New World Order has been prompted recently by the precipitate fall of communism. While the collapse of communism had not been anticipated by much of the world, Islamic literature had, for several decades, criticized both communism and capitalism and expected neither to endure. In their comparative works Muslim scholars have clearly demonstrated how and where each of these systems fall short in comparison with an independent system based on the teachings of Islam.

It would be rash to conclude that the collapse of communism attests to the fitness of capitalism. Both are flawed because they are materialistic ideologies unsuited for a species whose characteristics extend far beyond the material. Another fallacy of these ideologies—albeit in opposite directions—is the assumption that the individual and the society are in irreconcilable conflict. Communism sought to crush the individual in favor of society. Yet what is society but the individual multiplied? The result was inevitably a crushed society.

Capitalism, on the other hand, extols individuality and unduly shields it from the claims of society. This has imbued the individual with a sense of justifiable selfishness, and when this sense has been projected outward, its various expressions have been classism, corporatism, nationalism, racism, slavery and colonialism. The cornerstone of capitalism is that the only function and sole destiny of capital is to grow and keep growing without limits. When local markets are fully saturated, new ones are sought overseas and in the

Third World. There is obvious (or, perhaps, willful) blindness to the fact that it is impossible to attain infinite growth on a finite planet.

The feverish race for dollars and more dollars is coupled with the planned and active encouragement of patterns of consumerism and planned obsolescence—not to satisfy needs, but rather to satisfy the wish for comforts, pleasures, and luxuries. Natural resources, many irreplaceable, are being violated at an accelerating pace. This drive for overkill has targeted, as its sacrificial lamb, the world's resources. It has especially exploited the Third World, a vital market and cheap source of labor and materials, which it presumes to be expendable. Not only are its peoples stripped of their natural resources and raw materials for a meager price (compared to the exorbitant prices they pay to buy the finished products of those materials), they are even prevented from carrying out such projects that might improve their lot and make them less dependent on First World imports.

To prevent the Third World from total death by exsanguination, it is regularly injected with fresh capital in the form of loans and aid in order to maintain its buying power, to the favor of Western capital.

Alas, only a tiny fraction of that aid goes to address the needs of the people. The major part goes to the home-grown elite, who form the ruling class, and their retinues, who undertake the maintenance of the status quo. They prevent the public debate of the terms and conditions of the loans and aid, and block any attempt at supervising their management and establishing accountability for their mismanagement. They oppress labor rights and allow lax safety procedures, and keep

a total ban on unearthing the appalling corruption that
has become the hallmark of government in the Third
World—including much of the Islamic World. This
seems to explain two paradoxes. The first is that in
many Middle Eastern countries, the more money the
West pumps in, the poorer the country becomes and
the deeper it gets into debt. The second is the total
betrayal by the major democracies of the democratic
movements of the Middle East that seem close to gaining power through following sound democratic process. Invariably the democracies side with the dictators
against the democratic aspirations of the people, and,
when necessary, support dictators even with the use of
military power.

The expression *stability*, which is the declared aim
of every Western intervention, means in real terms the
reservation of the best exploitative opportunities for
foreign capital, even if they are the worst possible for
the foreign masses. They and future generations will
inherit a rising debt that their GNP is unable to service,
let alone pay. This state of affairs is both known and
bitterly felt by the people of the Third World. They
see its results in their homes, their families and in the
extremely limited opportunities available to their children. They call it injustice and they try to change it,
but they are brutally suppressed. Western politicians
participate in this suppression, and to justify it in the
eyes of their people, propagandistic formulae and ter-
minologies are promptly employed (such as declaring
that their victims are eroding the stability of their
nation or committing blatant aggression on our
national interests). Until recently, it was convenient to
call those seekers of justice "communists." Since the

collapse of communism, their new label is "Islamic fundamentalists."

Under the influence of a gigantic media machine, owned by large corporations and big capital, designed to manipulate and shape public thinking, the masses in the West have so far been swift to swallow the bait and, unsuspectingly, sanction the means and ways of their policy-makers. And yet, this is not the worst fault of the submissive and unsuspecting nature of the people in the West. What they have been even slower to grasp is that the voracious appetite of capital and its greedy practice in the Third World is not confined to those faraway places inhabited by strange and exotic people. Government and big business do not flinch from doing the same at home to their own citizens whenever prompted by the dictates of their sacred principle: growth and more growth, capital and more capital, dollars and more dollars! What else can explain the shifting of major chunks of industry to Southeast Asia and elsewhere, where cheap labor (financially and humanly) can produce a cheaper final product which, however, will not be sold cheaper when shipped back home to America? During the process, millions of American workers have been laid off and joined the ranks of the unemployed.

This road of unbridled capitalism cannot continue indefinitely. All evidence shows that it will hit a dead end before long, evidence that has been attacked, ignored, and even hidden, but it is there, whether its opponents like it or not. The twin golden-egged geese of the world's resources and peoples of the Third World shall not survive for long. Unless there is radical change before it is too late, this planet will eventually cease to be sustainable.

What is called for, however, is not merely a change of rules but a change of heart. As long as the mentality of materialism reigns, there is no hope for more than symptomatic treatment that might delay the inevitable for a brief time but will not prevent it. So long as the prevailing thinking views human interaction in terms of us versus them, North versus South, exploiter versus exploited, rich versus poor, white versus people of color, and masters versus slaves (or servants), there is no hope for the future. The ship of humanity will sink, even while the passengers in deluxe and first class cabins further amass more valuables and luxuries.

It is doubtful that the politicians and the financiers of the world possess the necessary vision, wisdom, and ability to undergo a dramatic self-change. It is pitiful to watch them staying the ominous course and leading humanity so close to the edge of the abyss. The only hope is a massive campaign to educate the public who, as voters, remain the final arbiters at the end of the day. If a demand is created for a new way, then politicians will either have to change or get out of the way of change.

What does Islam have to do with all this? Islamic scholars and thinkers (not the terrorists and extremists that the media hold as a fixed mask on the face of everything Islamic) have, for several decades, been sketching the features of an Islamic system that would address world problems and is based on the Islamic Shari'ah, which is naturally not a copy of formulas that might have served well in previous times and circumstances. Nor is this system to be considered exclusively Islamic or prescribed strictly for Muslims, for the welfare of humanity is a common concern and with our ever-shrinking interactive globe, we all face the same destiny. The principal features of this system are described below:

### The Authority Over Man

Man is not the supreme being of this universe, but is responsible and accountable to the Supreme Being, God! Without God everything becomes possible, as Dostoyevsky said, and anything can be rationalized and justified. When man dethroned God he slipped into self-worship. The true role of man in this universe is to be God's vicegerent and trustee, so equipped as to be capable of having full mandate over nature in order to manage the planet in accordance with the Creator's instructions, and not upon his own impulses and temptations. Neither science (a tool yet in its infancy) nor arrogance (a killer trap) should delude man into playing God . . .if only man were wise enough.

### The Ownership of Goods

Ultimate ownership is God's by virtue of His being the Creator. Our ownership is a secondary ownership. We are free to own and to increase our wealth by lawful means, practically without limits, so long as we are aware that capital not only has rights but also duties. The function of capital is not merely to grow ad infinitum, but also to fulfil obligations towards society.

The assumption (by both communism and capitalism) that there is an inevitable conflict between the individual and society does not exist in Islam, in which the premise is an equilibrium that is delicately balanced between both and does justice to all. This balance is not maintained merely by the strong arm of the law, but by a strong desire to win God's pleasure that makes giving a continuous source of joy for the giver. God is always in the equation and is a living reality, a notion that, from a materialistic perspective, is irrelevant and absolutely meaningless.

In Islam the premise is that God has remitted the sustenance of the poor in the wealth of the rich—and in a new world order, the principle may be carried over to international proportions. This new system is of course achievable and attainable, but not under a value-free educational system, a tidal wave of media indoctrination, or a society tolerant of injustices. Society is now so interdependent and integrated that nobody can live in isolation, either at the apex of riches or at the nadir of poverty.

Over fourteen centuries ago Omar, the second caliph of Islam, decreed that if a man died in poverty, the citizens of his town had to pay his ransom as if they had killed him. The community is "like one body. . .when one organ suffers, the others rally in support," as the Prophet said. Every citizen has the right to live at a minimum level of comfort (not merely at subsistence level), and since living on charity is discouraged, it follows that individual rights include the right to gainful employment. Labor-saving technology is therefore allowed as an answer to a labor shortage, but never to economize on jobs and throw laborers into unemployment. Man takes priority over machine, and the juridical rule is that the collective welfare takes priority over individual welfare. This does not mean the arrest of technological progress, but that it should go hand in hand with labor in dealing with its consequences.

Workers are encouraged and supported in buying shares in their companies in order to blur the polarization between labor and capital and to enable them to have a vested interest in the progress of their companies.

Another rule in Islam is that money as an instrument cannot breed money unless coupled to some kind of production; hence, usury is unlawful in Islam. In recent decades much has been written on usury-free banking, and indeed a number of banks, not only in Islamic countries but also in Europe and America, have successfully pioneered its application.

### The Equality of Man

The *oneness* of humanity as a single family sharing the common grandparentage of Adam and Eve should be emphasized and taught to children from a young age, together with the concept of the inherent equality of human beings. It is unfortunate that both science and religion were, at one time, misused in Europe (and America) to concoct evidence of the natural superiority of the white (or Aryan) race over the others. The false evidence in support of this claim is now dead and buried, but its legacy continues. In most churches in the West until now, Jesus is portrayed as a blond white man with blue eyes, unlike the brunet, olive-complexioned people common in the area of Palestine.

The evidence of racism in the West practically pervades all aspects of life, and the will to change it is yet to gather sufficient momentum. An uphill battle for civil rights in America has been going on for decades, and in spite of palpable progress, one cannot say that the bitter taste of slavery has been washed away.

Equality is not a set of legal specifications but is primarily a state of mind.

So far the black man in America has not heard the word "sorry" from the white man for the chapter of slavery that tarnished the history of white civilization (although the non-white Japanese Americans did receive an apology and reparations for their internment during World War II). Racial tensions continue to erupt, and although regrettable, the participants in these incidents of violence often have some justification. The Los Angeles riots in the near past[14] are a case in point.

Every time there is a call for action to improve the lot of American blacks, the response, though often helpful for a limited time, usually misses the root cause of the problem. Neither bullets nor dollars will come up with permanent and real solutions. Only when everyone in the depths of their hearts feels and believes that every other human being is a dear and equal brother or sister will real change occur. This cannot be decreed by law, but is a function of education. To transform our world, we must bring about a total educational revolution with the objective of creating a unified and compassionate society, undivided by barriers of any kind, and giving new life and significance to slogans of freedom, fraternity, and equality, not only within national borders, but on a global scale.

To effect change, the re-education of the neo-colonialist nations must be coupled with a real effort on their part to assist the development of the Third World. It has been estimated that the subsidy Europe pays to its farmers is enough to cause such a

---

[14] April of 1992.

turnaround in the Third World as to eliminate the problem of hunger the world over. Such an idea was summarily scoffed at in a (philanthropic) meeting in Europe of former ministers and prime ministers from various countries. Neither the elimination of subsidy nor the development of the Third World were considered live options, the former for reasons of political expediency and the latter for political strategy.

### The Need for Self-restraint

Application of the uniquely human faculty of self-restraint has been rapidly eroding and needs to be restored. Although it is a principal distinction between man and animal, the mentality of modern times seems to have played havoc with it. A young man who was arrested for shooting at passing cars on a freeway and killing some people had only this to offer as explanation: "I felt like killing someone." This is not a lone example. Statistics on crime clearly indicate that grossly impulsive and destructive behavior has become a common social phenomenon rather than an exception, as anyone who watches the news or reads the papers can confirm. The lack of a sound value system and the consequent appalling lack of resistance in the face of impulses and temptations are underlying factors that have led to gradual societal destruction.

A key to change can be found with education and the media—but education must be informed not only by knowledge but also by a belief in what is right and an awareness that we are accountable to a higher power—only then will most people become fully responsive to the promptings of their conscience. If there is a Day of Judgment, as Muslims and others believe, then one cannot envy the media moguls who will be confronted by their role in publicizing and promoting violence, pornography and licentiousness. Speak lightly of the unthinkable and it naturally becomes thinkable. Our young then explore and experiment until debauchery and miscreancy become societal addictions.

Unfortunately, some states are subtly setting the example to their youth of recourse to naked power, especially when they are strong beyond limits and their adversaries are weak beyond limits. The fig leaf called values and principle often falls when the military giants crack down on presumed aggression with all their might and practically against no resistance; when a worse aggression follows, the same giants pull back because "the task would not be easy." Regard for human life is abysmal, both as they attack it or refrain from protecting it. One of the powerful but revealing comments made by a military leader during the Gulf War was, "We are not in the business of counting bodies," but he, of course, meant the bodies of the other side.

### War and Peace

The rules of war in Islam are very clear and were explicitly delineated by Prophet Muhammad himself. It must either be of a defensive nature or to remove oppression wherever it might be, following what is now called a just cause, and it must be fought without harm to innocent civilians or the environment. Alliance to stop aggression is expressed in the Quranic verse: *"If two parties among the believers fall into a fight, make peace between them, but if one of them transgresses against the other, then fight (all) against the one that transgresses until it complies with the command of God.*

*But if it complies, then make peace with justice and be fair, for God loves those who are fair"* (49:9).

Alliance with non-Muslims for a just cause is acceptable. An example is the Prophet's treaty with the Jews of Madinah to defend that city jointly from the disbelievers. Another example is the reference by the Prophet to a treaty made between the tribes of Makkah long before Islam, who agreed to join together in supporting the oppressed. The Prophet commented, "That was an alliance before Islam, but if, in Islam, I had been invited to it, I would have joined it." The Prophet's explicit instructions to his armies were strict in that they should fight only against belligerents and not against women, children, or the elderly. Non-Muslim religious people in their monasteries or houses of worship also should not be harmed, nor should enemy trees be cut or set on fire as a war measure, nor should animals be targeted or slaughtered except for food. When one reviews these stipulations, it becomes obvious that the implementation of these lofty Islamic war ethics requires a special effort in a modern war. Perhaps World War I was the last war in which it was possible for fighting to be fairly confined to military personnel. Starting with the Spanish Civil War in the thirties, the rules began to change as was evident in World War II, the Korean War and the Vietnam War. The two atomic bombs over Hiroshima and Nagasaki speak for themselves, as does the carpet bombing of the Vietnam war and its "free fire zones," killing not only people, animals and plants, but even the soil itself.

Some people would therefore take it that those Islamic war ethics are now theoretical and cannot hold in our modern age. Muslims and others, however, look at the issue from another perspective. Since modern

warfare is so devastating, war itself should cease to be
an option in conflict resolution. War should be obsolete
just like slavery! It is a bad omen that the New World
Order was announced on the occasion of an overwhelm-
ing military strike. Subsequent decisions raise suspicion
that what is new in the New World Order is no more
than the old order presided over by one adversary
instead of two.

With humanity at the present apex of civilization—
never attained before—and ready to move into the
second millennium heralding and celebrating a New
World Order, a world free of war, and with some alternate instruments of just peacemaking, is no longer an
idle dream.

Why can't independent courts of justice settle differences between nations? After all, war does not differentiate between right and wrong but only shows
who is stronger and possesses more destructive power.
The implementation of fair and just conflict resolution
would be quite possible if courts of law capable and
desirous of honest and impartial handling of conflict
were established (this excludes the United Nations and
its Security Council). The success of any such proposal revolves totally around one pivot: that the civilized
countries decide to be civilized! It takes truth, and
nobody would ever say they are against truth, but they
are. Truth is a value, and regrettably politics are blind
to values, and this is the real threat that we face today.

Will the strong accede to justice as decided by law
or persist in believing that might makes right? Will the
military-industrial complex give up its *raison d'etre,*
justifying itself by some war or another every now and
then? Can justice be accepted in apportioning the

cake of the world resources and the cost of replenishing them? Of course not; that would be blasphemous to the masters of the current order, unless things change, and change will not come from above. It will come from below upwards, from the grass roots.

### The Ecology

For the sake of making dollars to buy their food, service their debts, arm their military, protect their dictators and satisfy the insatiable appetite of their rulers and elite, the poorer side of humanity in the developing countries are condemned to deplete their natural resources. On the part of the affluent side of humanity, with the goal of making the rich richer to enhance their consumeristic patterns, increase their luxuries and indulge in their pleasantries, the industrialized world is violating, poisoning, polluting and killing the ecology. This happens at a time when science and technology are capable of influencing the biosphere in a dramatic and unprecedented way, and it happens in peace time, apart from the devastating and permanent damage that a full scale modern war is capable of causing. We borrow from the future at an extravagant rate, whereas sane and reasonable estimates tell us that we are incurring a debt our future generations will not be able to pay. Remedial measures and workable suggestions have been prescribed, but the obstacle, as expected, has been those who hold the reins of power, the custodians of unbridled, greedy, selfish, gluttonous, short-sighted capitalism. As the Quran says, *"There is the type of man whose speech about this world's life may dazzle you, and he calls God to be his witness about what is in his heart, yet is he the most contentious of enemies. When he prevails, he goes about the earth spreading mischief and destroying tilth and progeny; and God loves not mischief"* (2:204-205).

Notwithstanding bitter opposition from big business, the ecology movement outside the sphere of politics has steadily gained momentum. On Earth Day 1990, one hundred million people in 140 countries showed up for the largest grass-roots demonstration ever. This cannot be ignored by the politicians who would otherwise lose their votes. Perhaps it is time to establish an international ecological agency in which world governments would participate with the prior agreement to voluntarily heed its recommendations, recommendations that, of course, should not be oblivious to the question of justice.

### Population Issues

The world population is growing at a pace which far exceeds that of available resources. Concerns about the population explosion are therefore quite legitimate. Since most of the population increase occurs in the Third World, the latter has been accused of irresponsible behavior and targeted for blame by the West. Disciplinary action has been considered, and a number of countries that provide aid, including the United States of America, have entertained the idea of linking that aid with fertility regulation and family planning achievements. Worse than that, in an article entitled "Would Machiavelli now be a better guide for doctors than Hippocrates?"[15] Dr. Jean Martin reviews some Western opinions that question the advisability of some

---

[15] *World Health Forum*, vol. 14, 1993, 105.

vaccination programs and other health measures in the Third World, since they allow too many children to live and utilize resources, which eventually causes the cycle of famine and death to be repeated. In other words, there is a call to setting limits on the reduction of mortality in the Third World. A shift from humanitarianism to "pragmatism" sounds logical to some, hence the inclusion of Machiavelli's name in the article.

That there is a problem, no one can deny. That there is need to avail families who wish to use them (without coercion) of safe, reliable and accessible contraceptive methods is a fact also, and Islam has no qualms with that. Our only reservation is that putting the blame of the population problem solely and squarely on Third World countries is not telling the whole truth, for the issue is really multifaceted. Placing blame on the Third World ignores the fact that the birth of one baby in the United States ". . .imposes more than a hundred times the stress on the world resources and environment as a birth in, say, Bangladesh," wrote Paul and Anne Ehrlich of the Department of Biological Sciences at Stanford University, in *National Geographic Magazine*. They note that while population problems in poor nations keep them poor, population problems in rich nations are destroying the ability of the earth to support civilization.[16]

The way to reduce population growth in the Third World has been debated (especially at the World Population Conference in Bucharest, 1974). Historical precedent (studying what happened in Europe that

---

[16] Quoted in Michael Henderson, *Hope for a Change* (Salem: Grosvenor Books, 1991), 24.

brought down fertility rates) and common sense indicate that development is the cause and not the outcome of reduced fertility—development is the best pill. That insecurity is a natural stimulus of fertility is also a known phenomenon. Yet the capitalist countries put a disproportionately high emphasis on fertility regulation in the Third World. Their concern goes far beyond mere philanthropic or altruistic considerations for the welfare of humanity.

In the summer 1991 issue of *Foreign Affairs,* a report (originally prepared for the US Army Conference on Long Range Planning) by Dr. Nicholas Eberstadt of the American Enterprise Institute warns against the implications of the proportional increase in numbers in the Third World nations for the international political order and the balance of world power. After three generations, he notes, eight great-grandparents in the West will share only four or five descendants against over three hundred for much of Africa and the Middle East; therefore, the leading countries of today will be the smallest nations in the future.

The National Security Study Memorandum 200, a study of "Implications of Worldwide Population Growth for US Security and Overseas Interests,"[17] is a very educative document, revealing the complex political, economic and military implications and the solid realities of the world in which we live. Population factors might be the seeds of revolutionary actions and an impetus for the expropriation or limitation of foreign economic interests. Poverty, population growth, and

---

[17] National Archives. Files of the National Security Study Memorandum 200. RG 273.

population youth[18] would urge development, induce the review of foreign investment terms and conditions and even boost military growth if conscription to the military is seen as a viable alternative to unemployment. The document at times imparts the feeling that industrial countries are already waging a pre-emptive war against underdeveloped countries.

It would seem to us that a New World Order should be geared to the needs of the global village, for that is what our planet is becoming. It should not presuppose the inevitability of dividing the world into haves and have-nots, and hence the inevitability of a fight to the death between them. It requires of the rich to be humble, content and willing to give up for the common good many luxuries that their current lifestyles incorporate. Their luxuries are not vital necessities, their reward would the happiness of providing the vital necessities for the major part of the human family. What else can be more conducive to happiness? God must be brought to the equation!

## JIHAD

The word *jihad* has been frequently used by the Western press over the past few decades, explained directly or subtly to mean "holy war." In point of fact, the term "holy war" was coined in Europe during the

---

[18] The common phenomenon in Third World countries in which the majority of a nation's population is young, resulting from an accelerated birth rate, especially among the young, and a lower life expectancy than in developed nations. Ed.

Crusades, meaning the war against Muslims. It does not have a counterpart in the Islamic glossary, and *jihad* is certainly not its translation.

*Jihad* means "striving." In its primary sense it is an inner struggle, within the self, to rid it from debased actions or inclinations and to exercise constancy and perseverance in achieving a higher moral standard. Since Islam is not confined to the realm of the individual but extends to the welfare of society and humanity in general, a Muslim cannot strive to improve himself or herself in isolation from what happens in his or her community or in the world at large, hence the Quranic injunction to the Islamic nation to take as a duty *"to enjoin good and forbid evil"* (3:104). It is a duty that is not exclusive to Muslims but applies to the human race, which is, according to the Quran, God's vicegerent (deputy) on earth. Muslims, however, cannot shirk this responsibility even if others do. The means to fulfil it are varied, and in our modern world encompass all legal, diplomatic, arbitrative, economic, and political instruments.

Islam does not exclude the use of force by which to curb evil, if there is no viable alternative. A forerunner of the collective security principle and collective intervention to stop aggression, at least in theory, as manifested in the United Nations Charter, is the Quranic reference, *"...make peace between them (two fighting groups), but if one of the two persists in aggression against the other, fight the aggressors until they revert to God's commandment"* (49:9). Military action is therefore a subgroup of jihad and not its totality. This was what Prophet Muhammad emphasized to his companions when, returning from a military campaign, he told them, "This day we have returned from the minor jihad (war) to the major jihad (self-control and betterment)."

Jihad is not a declaration of war against other religions and is certainly not directed against Christians and Jews, as some media and political circles want it to be perceived. Islam does not fight against other religions. Christians and Jews are considered as fellow inheritors of the Abrahamic traditions by Muslims, worshipping the same God and following the tradition of Abraham.

The rigorous criteria for a "just war" in Islam have already been alluded to, as well as the moral and ethical constraints that should be abided by. Modern warfare does not lend itself to those moral standards; therefore, war should be replaced by some other alternative for conflict resolution, if all sides agree on a just formula. An enlightened and resolute world public opinion could overcome and subdue war-oriented mentalities. The key is a change of heart. Just as there is a constructive role for forgiveness in interpersonal relations, so might this be possible in international relations provided justice, and not force, is the final arbiter.

We must reiterate for the sake of honesty that historically peoples of all traditions, Muslim, Christian, and Jewish, as well as others, have had their lapses in honestly following the valued ideals of their religions or philosophies. We have all made mistakes and we will continue to do so. Muslims are no exception, and time and again religion has been exploited by ambitious tyrants or violated by ignorant mobs. This is no reflection on religion, but it shows how desperately humanity is in need of better education, more enduring concern for human dignity, rights and freedoms, and vigilant pursuit of justice, even at the price of curbing political and economic greed.

## FAMILY AND THE SEXUAL REVOLUTION

Prophet Muhammad said: "Women are the other half of men." The unit of humanity is not a man or a woman. It is a man and a woman united in marriage that makes them a family (just like the smallest part of water is not oxygen or hydrogen, but both united). Like Judaism, Christianity, and many other religions, Islam decrees that the pairing off of a man and a woman to form a family constitutes a sacred bond that the Quran calls "a solemn pledge," which must be documented and authenticated by the marriage contract, or wedlock.

Marriage signifies the commitment of spouses to each other and establishes their mutual rights and responsibilities as well as those vis-a-vis their children. Children have the right to legitimacy (to know the identity of and benefit from a relationship with both their parents, as well as to be born within a valid marriage); to loving care as they are raised; to both physical and spiritual nurturing; and to education, to enable them to face life and bear its responsibilities as mature and useful citizens.

As parents attain old age or become incapacitated in some way, it is then their children's religious duty to look after them and cater to their comfort without showing their impatience in fulfilling this obligation.

This is a right owed to God and perpetual insurance as well, for it will one day benefit those children themselves, as they become parents, attain old age, and need the care of their own children.

The solidarity of the family and strength of family ties is of paramount importance in Islam. It spreads even beyond the nuclear family, along the widening circles of blood ties. The Quran calls it "the relation of the womb." It is both a duty and a rewardable charity to be kind to blood kindred through friendly care or financial support if needed. After parents have died, it remains one's duty to pray for them and even to maintain ties with their friends, show them courtesy, and offer help if needed.

In Islam, marriage subserves two functions, and it is only marriage that lawfully subserves them. The one is to fulfil the yearning of the one half to its other half and their becoming one, both physically and spiritually: *"Amongst His signs is that He created for you, from amongst you, consorts, with whom to dwell in tranquility; and He placed love and compassion between you"* (30:21). The other function is to procreate and have progeny: *"God made for you, from amongst you, consorts, and out of your consorts made for you children and grandchildren, and bestowed on you from His bounty; would they then believe in vain things and deny the blessings of God?"* (16:72).

Marriage is the only legitimate venue for sex and reproduction. Trespassing outside marriage is a grave sin, and it can also be a legal offense in Islam if witnessed by four witnesses who identify the perpetrators and testify to having seen the actual sexual union of a couple (not merely the appearance or possibility of their having sex, assumed because of their posture or otherwise). The legal criteria necessary for witnesses to accuse a person of adultery are stringent and serve to virtually preclude the possibility of false accusation in a matter so serious as this, having the potential to destroy the family unit.

It is noteworthy that the moral principles of chastity before marriage and fidelity thereafter formerly prevailed in America and the West, but with the slippage of more and more people into atheism or microtheism, change was inevitable. Atheism is when God is denied. Microtheism is when God is acknowledged, but with greatly reduced reverence. We worship Him, but on our own terms. We visit the houses of worship, usually on weekends, but we do not allow God out to tell us what to do with our private or public lives. This erosion of faith set the stage for the "sexual revolution," as all religious values became subject to radical revision.

The sexual revolution did not begin as recently as the nineteen sixties, as many suppose. Nor was it the outcome of a passive, natural social change; it was a consequence of the well-planned and persistent efforts of those who wished for change in societal mores regarding sex. It all started with society's extreme fascination with science and its technological capabilities, in the wake of banishment of the church from delving into public life. In the belief that science had finally dethroned religion as the source of true knowledge, many considered the human mind the ultimate arbiter of all human affairs, and all time-honored values were subjected to its new rulings. In their haste and superficiality, however, people missed the obvious fact that the human mind itself, and by its own admission, is an imperfect instrument, and that with its limitations it cannot pass such ultimate judgments as those concerning absolute moral standards. The mere fact that man continually and diligently seeks more knowledge and pursues further research is a confession that there is so much we yet need to learn. Had we really believed that we possessed all knowledge and that our minds were perfect, we should have ceased all research geared toward gaining more and more knowledge of our life and surroundings; we would then no longer have to spend on lavish research budgets. This, however, is not the case, for as the Quran says, *"Of knowledge, it is only a little that was communicated to you (the human race)"* (17:85).

To further replace God by man, between the two world wars a movement arose called "Morality without Religion," accusing religion—not human error—of causing enmity and conflict between people. Members of that movement assumed that high moral standards could be attained without necessarily ascribing them to religion and called those standards "unattached moralities." While few officially belonged to this movement, the philosophy it espoused gradually became more prevalent as people lost confidence in religion because of discrepancies between the Bible and scientific findings. As religion moved out of focus, God was dethroned, and new codes of morality were issued wherein the immoralities of yesterday became the normalities of today, and secular humanism could at last frankly declare that human values must be determined by human beings and without reference to any non-human or supernatural criterion. With the shift towards materialism, such values as honor, chastity

and purity became empty words and non-viable cur-
rency. A full range of indoctrination worked to stretch
the boundaries of freedom to include license, and in a
society that emphasized individuality, every human
whim then became a human right.

It was another setback for morality when the tidal
wave that hit society deluged also many of the traditional custodians of religion and its values—the clergy.
The affected clergy became a Trojan horse, because
instead of leaving the religious camp to join the liber-
tarians, they started working on religion itself, con-
structing new re-interpretations and exegeses of the
texts to render lawful and permissible what had been
unlawful and reprehensible throughout the entire history of religion. Many of these clergy themselves fell
prey to the germs they were supposed to fend off.
Some even interpreted the institution of celibacy as
refraining from marriage but not from having sex.[19]

The result, as expected, is the chaotic sexual conduct
of whole societies. Without the values of chastity outside marriage and fidelity within it came the desecration
of sex as a very special bond between a man and a
woman, widespread promiscuous sex, rapes, unwanted
pregnancies ending in abortion or unwanted children
stripped of their right of legitimate double parentage,
and children begetting children. Further, family trust is
eroded when even among stable families some fifteen
percent of children are illegitimate. Added to all this
are health hazards due to the epidemic spread of sexual-
ly transmitted diseases, whether new diseases or the

---

[19] Keith L. Woodward et al., "Gays in the Clergy," *Newsweek*,
February 23, 1987, 58.

recurrence of old ones we thought had been conquered long ago, the causative organisms of which have acquired resistance to known antibiotic therapy, and which are exacting a heavy toll on society, especially the youth, because of increased promiscuity.

Muslims do not have any confusion or vagueness about what is lawful in our religion and what is unlawful. The Quran remains in the original form that was revealed, word for word and letter for letter. The Quran is the divine word (any translation or rendition in any language, including Arabic [the Quranic language], cannot be called Quran). The moralities and the immoralities specified in the Quran will remain so forever, and cannot be diluted, manipulated, or rationalized. There are no clergy or scholars who can claim to be endowed with the right or ability of special interpretation. This does not mean that all Muslims are therefore virtuous people who do not sin. Of course, some Muslims violate their own religion by committing sins and abominations, but at least they know it is sin, and it will remain on their conscience until they desist and repent to God.

A real challenge in the promotion of morality faces those Muslims who are citizens of non-Muslim communities where their children are surrounded by social and moral norms that conflict with the teachings of Islam. Muslims are not alone in this, because there are also Jews, Christians and others who uphold similar divine moralities and make every effort to impart belief in them to their children. Cooperation toward this end is already in progress and more is encouraged between Muslims and those who believe similarly, be they clergy, lay individuals or associations.

Our way with our children follows an early introduction to God (see chapter one) and to the concept
that belief in Him means we accept and abide by His
rules. If we follow His rules we do not bother if others
do not, for when one is on the side of God, then one is
in the majority, since the whole of His creation is similarly subservient to His laws.

Faith breeds the confidence that resists peer pressure and the vagaries of temptation. "They all do it"
ceases to be an excuse. This "vaccination approach,"
grounding children in the knowledge of faith, aims at
building up their immunity long before they are
exposed to disease, be it physical or moral. Just as a
soldier is prepared to fight before and not during a battle, future hazards are discussed with a child so that he
or she can decide in advance what position to take
when the time comes, whether asked to take part in
smoking, drink, drug, or sex.

The preaching of premarital chastity entails more
than an order to obey (although of course, the teaching
is that when God orders, we hear and we obey).
Discussions with Muslim and non-Muslim youth can
present the case powerfully, although along purely intellectual lines. Asked "Who believes in equality of the
sexes?" and it is a unanimous vote in favor. "Who
believes in justice?" and again it is a unanimous agreement. The proposition is then introduced that any relationship between two partners, the consequences of
which are not equally shared by both, cannot constitute
justice; they all agree. In a situation of liberal sex, the
consequences are not equally shared, because the female
side is the loser all the way, whether she is deserted, gets
pregnant and has an abortion, or gives birth and signs

away her baby for adoption or ends up with a fatherless baby to support alone for the rest of her life. When the consequences are observed and the question is asked, "Can this be justice?" the general shout is "No!"

The homosexuality movement was a fairly late arrival at the scene of the sexual revolution. Homosexuality, of course, is not a new invention and has existed in practically all cultures and among all people, but usually in far fewer numbers than today. Its influence has mushroomed only over the past decade or so through lobbying and other organized promotional efforts. I do remember attending academic conferences in which some scientific papers were presented, using scientific methodology to "prove" by scientific experiment the safety of anal sex. This was in the early seventies, and to me the findings were so contradictory to simple common sense that I began, for the first time in my academic life, to doubt the honesty of some scientific researchers. Shortly thereafter, the American Psychiatric Association declared that homosexuality was no longer to be considered an illness, but was to be regarded as merely an orientation or a sexual variant. The rest is history.

A "Gay Bowel Syndrome" was later described in the medical literature, and later it was AIDS that made the news, and its relation to homosexual behavior was established. Very soon the AIDS problem was pushed out of the medical arena, which was unable to impose upon it its usual rules and regulations for containment of infectious diseases. AIDS became a political issue, and the homosexual lobby grew into a political power capable of intimidating office-bearers and political figures and gaining the support of many in the media, the arts and the clergy. Instead of AIDS being contained it spilled over, affecting blood recipients, drug addicts, the fetus in utero, heterosexual contacts with wives (and others), and those who have inadvertently come into contact with contaminated bodily fluids. It has become a global epidemic and is spreading at a serious pace. For the AIDS patient, Muslims have empathy, compassion, and hopefully the best available medical care. To those not infected, we recommend the preventive approach. This is not the condom, for there is no such thing as safe sex. The only safe sex is chastity until marriage and fidelity within marriage.

The debate about homosexuality is raging. "Be what you are," it is said, "and do not be ashamed of it." Many unsuspecting youth then start to experiment, to "discover" what they really are. Consent is a prerequisite, and lobbies in Scandinavia are trying to bring down the age of consent to four years. A 'Gay Pride Day' is annually observed in California with media coverage, a 'Gay Pride Month' in some school districts has been established to remove bigotry and prejudice, and two-man or two-woman households are being presented as alternative forms of family.

Recently, science began exploring a possible anatomical or genetic basis for homosexual orientation. Muslims are not impressed, and to us the matter is this simple: We do not make our religion, but we receive it and we obey it. We cannot impose our beliefs on anyone, but we believe in the veracity of the teachings of the Quran and of Prophet Muhammad that clearly and explicitly condemn homosexual practices. Whether one has the orientation or not, whether one thinks that one harbors the "homosexual gene" or not, one's feelings and desires cannot dictate behavior. You might be dying to do something (be it homosexual contact, heterosexual contact with a partner who is not your spouse, taking an alcoholic drink or committing a violent crime or theft), but what you feel need not be what you do. *"It is not for a believing man or woman, if a matter has been decided by God and His messenger, to have a choice of their own. If anyone disobeys God and His messenger, he is indeed on a clearly wrong path"* (33:36). Every human being has an undisputed gene without which they cannot be a human being: it is called the "gene of self-control."

# BIOMEDICAL ETHICS

REPRODUCTIVE ISSUES
   Fertility Regulation
      *Contraception*
      *Breast-feeding*
      *The intrauterine device*
      *Abortion*
      *Sterilization*
   Treatment of Infertility
      *Artificial insemination*
      *In vitro fertilization*
      *Surrogate motherhood*

ORGAN DONATION AND
TRANSPLANTATION
      *Transplantation of nervous tissue*
      *The anencephalic fetus*
      *Transplantation of sex glands*

DEFINITION OF DEATH

EUTHANASIA

GENETIC ENGINEERING

This section elucidates the Islamic perspective on subjects that have been at the forefront of the field of bioethics, and on which Islamic consensus has been fairly established.

## REPRODUCTIVE ISSUES

### Fertility Regulation

*Contraception.* Islam permits contraception so long as it does not entail the radical separation of marriage from its reproductive function. Since the time of the Prophet contraception has been practiced, but he made it clear that its use should be a joint decision between husband and wife. The general recommendation is for the Islamic nation to procreate and increase in number, but quality and not sheer numbers was emphasized by Muhammad. One of his very prophetic predictions was, "There will come a day when other nations will fall upon you like hungry eaters upon a bowl of food." When asked whether this would be due to lack of numbers, he said, "No. On that day you will be so many, but (in quality) you will be like the froth on the surface of a torrent."

Throughout Islamic history jurists have permitted family planning for a number of reasons, ranging from matters of health and socioeconomic ability to women's concern for the preservation of their beauty. Both natural and artificial methods of contraception are acceptable, provided they are not harmful and do not work as abortifacients. The use of contraception should be the choice of each individual family, without coercion or pressure. Countries that adopt a population policy may resort to wide campaigns of education to ensure the accessibility of contraceptive technology, but the decision must rest with the family.

Reservations about population programs designed by Western countries for the Third World were referred to earlier. Those in the Third World are aware of "demographic warfare," intended to strip their populations of sheer power of numbers or to reduce majorities to minorities in some areas. They are alarmed by the fact that contraceptive material that is banned from use in the (Western) countries in which it is produced is being abundantly exported to Islamic and Third World countries, compromising on safety standards. More investment on the part of the West remains to be seen in developing indigenous resources of the Third World and a willingness to transfer, toward that end, necessary technology.

*Breast-feeding.* Breast-feeding is strongly encouraged by Islamic teachings. As a family planning method it is not a reliable prescription for the individual family, but it has been estimated that on a group (collective) basis it is a more potent contraceptive than all other methods combined, measured by the drop in the fertility rate in communities of suckling women. The Quran mentions breast-feeding and that its natural course is a span of two years.

In Islam breast-feeding is regarded as more than a nutritional (or family planning) process. It is a "value" and is recognized as forging a special bond, so much so that a woman other than the natural mother who breast-feeds an infant acquires a special status in Islamic law, called "suckling parenthood," and this woman is called the infant's "mother in lactation." To accentuate its value, "lactation motherhood" is given the status of natural motherhood in legal rulings concerning marriage. The result is that such a mother's natural children are considered "lactation siblings" of the nursed infant, who therefore may not marry any of them.

*The intrauterine device (IUD).* If an intrauterine device serves as a contraceptive by actually causing abortion, it is not an acceptable method. The IUD no longer works by preventing implantation. Current generations of the device contain a copper wire that releases spermicidal copper ions, or include the hormone progesterone, which thickens the cervical mucus so that it cannot be penetrated by sperm. Both actions of these newer devices put the IUD in the category of contraception, not abortion; this has been confirmed by the World Health Organization.

*Abortion.* There are no "pro-life" and "pro-choice" lobbies in Islamic communities. Islam views abortion as being very different from contraception, since the former entails the violation of a human life. The question that naturally arises is whether the term "human life" includes the life of the fetus in the womb. According to Islamic jurisprudence, it does. Islam accords the fetus the status of "incomplete *dhimma.*" *Dhimma* is the legal regard that allows rights and duties, and that of the fetus is incomplete in the sense that it has rights but owes no duties. Some of the rights of the fetus are as follows:

1. If a husband dies while his wife is pregnant, the law of inheritance recognizes the fetus as an inheritor, if born alive. Other inheritors receive their shares in accordance with the prescribed juridical proportions, but only after the share of the unborn is set aside to await its birth.

2. If a fetus is miscarried at any stage of pregnancy and shows signs of life, such as a cough or movement, and then dies, such fetus has the right to inherit anything it was legally entitled to inherit from anyone who died after the beginning of the pregnancy. After this fetus dies, what it has inherited is inherited in turn by its legal heirs.

3. If a woman commits a crime punishable by death and is proven pregnant, then the execution of her punishment is postponed until she gives birth and nurses her baby until it is weaned. This applies irrespective of the duration of the

pregnancy, however early, denoting the right of the fetus to life from its beginning. It applies even if the pregnancy was illegitimate, which shows that the fetus conceived out of wedlock also has the right to life. All sects and juridical schools unanimously uphold this ruling.

4. There is a monetary penalty exacted for causing abortion, even if it is inadvertent. This is called the "ghorra." If aggression or willful action causes abortion, suitable punishment by the court is also imposed.

The question of the beginning of life has been discussed in Islamic circles since early times, since the inadmissibility of abortion is subject to establishing the existence of life (some past jurists permitted abortion before four months, others before seven weeks of pregnancy, on the assumption that life had not yet started in those stages of pregnancy). Some ten centuries ago, Al-Ghazali, a notable scholar, rightly described a phase of imperceptible life, before the phase that the mother could feel in the form of fetal quickening. Recent juridical congresses have reviewed the subject, taking into account the applications of modern technology, and concluded that the stage of an individual's life that can be called its beginning should satisfy *all* the following criteria: (1) it is a clear and well-defined event; (2) it exhibits the cardinal feature of life: growth; (3) if its growth is not interrupted, it will naturally progress through the subsequent stages of life as we know them; (4) it contains the genetic pattern that is characteristic of the human race at large, and also of a unique specific individual; and (5) it is not preceded by any other phase which combines the first four. Obviously, these postulates refer to fertilization.

Abortion is permitted, however, if the continuation of a pregnancy poses a serious threat to the mother. The Shari'ah considers the mother to be the root and the fetus to be the offshoot, the latter to be sacrificed if that is necessary to save the former. There are some who argue in favor of expanding the admissibility of abortion to also cover drastic cases of congenital anomalies and fetal illness incompatible with feasible life, if performed before a pregnancy is four months long.

*Sterilization.* Unless done for a clear medical indication, sterilization is generally frowned upon. It is permitted, however, for women with a reasonable number of children and who are approaching the end of their reproductive life. Voluntary and informed consent should be given by both the husband and wife, giving no promises of a guaranteed successful reversal of the operation if they later change their minds. No government policy should pressure people into undergoing sterilization. Doctors have the right to decline performing the operation if not convinced that it is in the best interests of the patient.

### Treatment of Infertility
The pursuit of pregnancy is legitimate and individuals may resort to taking necessary means toward that end, provided those means do not violate the Shari'ah.

*Artificial insemination.* Artificial insemination is permissible only if the sperm belongs to the husband

(AIH). Donor's semen (AID) may not be used since procreation is legitimate only within the marriage contract and the elements (the couple) that are party to it.

*In vitro fertilization (IVF)*. This procedure, commonly known as "test-tube-baby" technology, is Islamically acceptable so long as it is between husband and wife, i.e. within the boundaries of the marriage contract. The marriage contract should be valid and live. Since widowhood or divorce bring the marriage contract to a conclusion, it follows that a woman may not be impregnated by her deceased or ex-husband's sperm that is stored in a sperm bank. Inclusion of a third party other than husband and wife and the bearers of their genetic material (sperm and ovum) is not permissible because this would be an intrusion into the marriage contract that united the pair. "Alien sperm," an "alien egg," or an "alien womb" (to carry a couple's embryo) is not allowed.

*Surrogate motherhood*. Surrogate motherhood, in which a woman carries in her womb the fetus of another couple, is absolutely unacceptable in Islam. It entails a pregnancy outside the legitimacy of a marriage contract. It also results in the dichotomy of motherhood into genetic and biological components, whereas these should be one. Disagreement about parental rights between women involved in surrogacy has led to legal and other problems in America. A contract deciding the fate of the baby is certainly dehumanizing, as it treats the baby as a commodity. The implications might prove to be far-reaching and are not yet fully recognized, since never before in history have human females willingly chosen to undergo a full pregnancy and delivery with the prior intent of giving their babies to others. This is done, in the majority of cases, for a negotiated price, which reduces "motherhood" from a "value" to an asset. If this becomes established practice, its long-term effects on intergenerational bonds will be devastating.

## ORGAN DONATION AND TRANSPLANTATION

The Quran says: *". . .and whoever saves a life, it would be as if he saved the life of all the people."* Perhaps there is no better way to implement this concept than by transplanting donated organs in place of failing vital body parts. This conclusion was reached after some synthesis of Islamic rules.

Basically, violating the human body, whether living or dead, is against the rulings of Islam. It would follow that incising the body of a living donor or of a cadaver and obtaining an organ to be donated would be impermissible, had it not been for the invocation of two juridical rules that readily solve the impasse. The first is the rule, "Necessity overrules prohibition." The second is "The lesser of two evils should be chosen if both cannot be avoided." Since the saving of life is a necessity that carries more weight than preserving the integrity of the body or cadaver, and since injury to the body of a donor is less evil than leaving a patient to die, the procedure of organ donation and transplantation is sanctioned. It should not pose danger to the donor, as far as medically ascertainable. Rules of free consent, devoid of any kind of pressure, should be observed as a donor (or next of kin of a deceased donor) indicates his or her willingness.

*Transplantation of nervous tissue.* Recent experiments have shown some promise in the treatment of some diseases through the transplantation of nervous tissue. It is lawful if the source is the adrenal gland medulla or an animal fetus, or a human fetus spontaneously miscarried when it dies naturally. It is unlawful to sacrifice a living or viable human fetus for the purpose. In lawful abortion (such as to save the mother's life), tissue from the fetus may be used. Creating fetuses or performing abortion for the purpose of transplantation is unlawful.

*The anencephalic fetus.* An anencephalic fetus results from a congenital abnormality in which the vault of the skull and the brain hemispheres are absent. It might be born alive, but will eventually die after a variable period that might extend to several days. As long as it lives, it should not be used as a source of organs for transplantation. Artificial termination of its life is unlawful. It may be maintained by artificial resuscitation to keep its tissues healthy until its brain (stem) dies, and only then it is acceptable to take its organs.

*Transplantation of sex glands.* It is unlawful to transplant into another person testes capable of producing and discharging sperm or ovaries capable of ovulation, for this would lead to confusion of genealogy and the conception of babies by gametes that are not united by an authentic marriage, since such sperms and ova will always belong to the donor and not the recipient. Sex glands that are sterile (do not produce gametes) but are hormonally active do not bear this ban, but their use has no place in clinical practice.

### DEFINITION OF DEATH

The definition of the moment of death is obviously important to the resolution of medical issues, such as determining the permissibility of removing artificial animation or the taking of a singular vital organ for transplantation (such as the heart). Moreover, it has a direct bearing on juridical issues, such as the apportioning of legacy shares if two or more inheritors should die in succession, and determining the beginning of the waiting period a widow must wait after her husband's death before she remarries (four months and ten days, or, if pregnant, until the end of pregnancy).

Recent juridical congresses have accepted a new definition of death based on total brain death (including that of the brain stem), even while some physiological functions are maintained by artificial animation. The new definition was made possible through a process of "analogy" to an old juridical rule that recognized the concept of a fatal injury. Centuries ago, it was decreed that if a person was stabbed and that resulted in the extrusion of his bowel, that was a fatal injury, even if the victim continued to show movement and other signs of departing life, technically referred to as "the movement of the slain." If a second aggressor then finished up the victim causing (complete) death, the murder charge would still be addressed to the first aggressor, and the second would be charged, but not with murder. Persons with brain death whose body organs/systems remain, nevertheless artificially maintained, have been given the status of the "movement of the slain," seeing that return to life is scientifically impossible. It would be no crime, therefore, if animation was switched off in such a case, or if the (fresh and live) heart was taken from such a person for transplantation to a patient whose heart was damaged beyond recovery.

## EUTHANASIA

Euthanasia has gained a legal foothold in Holland. It went to the ballot box in two states in America but was defeated, although its lobby is becoming more active. Islam has its own definite views on euthanasia.

*Human life.* The sanctity of human life is a basic value as decreed by God even before the times of Moses, Jesus and Muhammad. Commenting on the slaying of Abel by his brother Cain (the two sons of Adam), God says in the Quran: *"On that account We ordained for the children of Israel that if anyone slay a person—unless it be for murder or spreading mischief in the land—it would be as if he slew the whole people. And if anyone saved a life, it would be as if he saved the life of the whole people"* (Quran 5:32). The Quran also says: *"Take not life, which Allah made sacred, otherwise than in the course of justice"* (Quran 6:151 and 17:33). The Shari'ah goes into great detail in defining the conditions under which taking life is permissible, whether in war or in peace (as an item of criminal law), with rigorous prerequisites and precautions to restrict its use.

*Is there a right to suicide?* Islam does not recognize suicide as a right, but rather considers it a violation. Since we did not create ourselves, we do not own our bodies. We are entrusted with them for care, nurture and safekeeping. God is the owner and giver of life and His rights in giving and in taking are not to be violated. Attempting to kill oneself is a crime in Islam as well as a grave sin. The Quran says: *"Do not kill (or destroy) yourselves, for verily Allah has been to you most Merciful"* (Quran 4:29).

To warn against suicide Prophet Muhammad said: "Whoever kills himself with an iron instrument will be carrying it forever in hell. Whoever takes poison and kills himself will forever keep sipping that poison in hell. Whoever jumps off a mountain and kills himself will forever keep falling down in the depths of hell."

*Euthanasia—"mercy killing"?* The Shari'ah has listed and specified the conditions that make the taking of a life permissible (i.e. exceptions to the general rule of the sanctity of human life), and they do not include "mercy killing" or make allowance for it. Human life has intrinsic value to be respected unconditionally, irrespective of other circumstances. The concept of a life not worthy of living does not exist in Islam.

Justification of taking life to prevent or escape suffering is not acceptable. Prophet Muhammad taught, "There was a man in older times who had an infliction that taxed his patience, so he took a knife, cut his wrist and bled to death. Upon this God said: 'My subject hastened his end, I deny him paradise.'" During one of the military campaigns, one of the Muslims was killed and the companions of the Prophet kept praising his gallantry and efficiency in fighting, but, to their surprise, the Prophet commented, "His lot is hell." Upon inquiry, the companions found out that the man had been seriously injured and so he supported the handle of his sword on the ground and plunged his chest onto its tip, committing suicide.

The Islamic Code of Medical Ethics[20] endorsed by the First International Conference on Islamic Medicine states, "Mercy killing, like suicide, finds no support except in the atheistic way of thinking that believes that our life on this earth is followed by void. The claim of killing for painful hopeless illness is also refuted, for there is no human pain that cannot be largely conquered by medication or by suitable neuro-surgery ...."

Furthermore, there is a transcendent dimension to the question of pain and suffering. Patience and endurance are highly regarded and highly rewarded values in Islam: "... *Those who patiently preserve will truly receive a reward without measure*" (Quran 39:10). "... *And bear in patience whatever (ill) may befall you; this, behold, is something to set one's heart upon*" (Quran 31:17).

Prophet Muhammad taught, "When the believer is afflicted with pain, even that of a prick of a thorn or more, God forgives his sins, and his wrongdoings are discarded as a tree sheds off its leaves."

When means of preventing or alleviating pain fall short, the spiritual dimension can be very effectively called upon to support the patient who believes that accepting and standing unavoidable pain will be to his or

---

[20] *Islamic Code of Medical Ethics* (Kuwait: Islamic Organization of Medical Sciences, 1981), 65.

her credit in the hereafter, the real and enduring life. To a person who does not believe in a hereafter this might seem insupportable, but to one who does, euthanasia is certainly insupportable.

*The financial factor.* There is no question that the financial cost of maintaining the incurably ill and the senile is a growing concern, so much so that some pro-euthanasia groups have gone beyond the concept of the "right to die" to that of the "duty to die." They claim that when the human machine has outlived its productive span, its maintenance is an unacceptable burden on the productive segment of society and it should be disposed of, abruptly, rather than allowing it to deteriorate gradually.[21]

This logic is completely alien to Islam. Values take priority over financial considerations. The care of the weak, old and helpless is a value in itself for which people should be willing to sacrifice time, effort and money, and this starts, naturally, with one's own parents: *"Your Lord decreed that you worship none but Him, and that you be kind to your parents. Whether one or both of them attain old age in your life, say not to them a word of contempt but address them in terms of honor. And lower to them the wing of humility out of compassion, and say: 'My Lord, bestow on them Your mercy even as they cherished me in childhood'"* (Quran 17:23-25). Because such care is a virtue ordained and rewarded by God in this world and in the hereafter,

---

[21] Atalli, Jacques. *La medicine en accusation.* Quoted in Michel Solomon, *'L' Avenir de la Vie,' Coll. Les Visages de L'avenir.* (Paris: Seghers, 1981), 273-275.

believers regard it not as a debit, but as an investment. In a materialistic, dollar-centric community this logic is meaningless, but not so in the value-oriented God-conscious community of the faithful.

When individual means cannot cover the cost of necessary care, it becomes, according to Islam, the collective responsibility of society, and financial priorities are reshuffled so that values take priority over pleasures (people actually derive more pleasure from heeding values than from pursuing other pleasantries). A prerequisite of this, of course, is the complete moral and spiritual re-orientation of a society that does not hold to these premises.

*Clinical situations.* In an Islamic setting the question of euthanasia does not usually arise, and if it does, it is dismissed as religiously unlawful. The patient should receive every possible psychological support and compassion from family and friends, including the patient's spiritual (religious) advisors. The doctor participates in this also and provides therapeutic measures for the relief of pain. A dilemma arises when the dose of the pain killer necessary to alleviate pain approximates or overlaps with the lethal dose that might bring about the patient's death. Ingenuity on the part of the doctor is called upon to avoid this situation, but from a religious point of view, the critical issue is the doctor's intention: is it to kill or to alleviate? Intention is beyond verification by the law, but according to Islam it cannot escape the ever-watchful eye of God, Who, according to the Quran, *"is aware of the [most] stealthy glance, and of all that the hearts conceal"* (Quran 40:19). Sins that cannot be proved to constitute a legal crime are beyond the domain of the judge but remain answerable to God.

The seeking of medical treatment for illness is mandatory in Islam, according to two sayings of the Prophet: "Seek treatment, subjects of God, for to every illness God has made a cure," and "Your body has a right on you." But when the treatment holds no promise, it ceases to be mandatory. This applies both to surgical and/or pharmaceutical measures, and, according to the majority of scholars, to artificial animation equipment. Ordinary needs that are the right of every living person and which are not categorized as "treatment" are regarded differently. These include food and drink and ordinary nursing care, and they are not to be withheld as long as the patient lives.

The Islamic Code of Medical Ethics (p.67), states: "In his or her defense of life, however, the doctor is well-advised to realize his limit and not transgress it. If it is scientifically certain that life cannot be restored, then it is futile to diligently keep the patient in a vegetative state by heroic means or to preserve the patient by deep freezing or other artificial methods. It is the process of life that the doctor aims to maintain and not the process of dying. In any case, the doctor shall not take a positive measure to terminate the patient's life."

### Commentary

The discussion of euthanasia cannot be isolated from the total ideologic background of any community. Muslims, believing in God and in a divinely prescribed Shari'ah, will naturally have different views on this issue from others who do not believe in God, or from those who acknowledge God but deny Him any authority to tell us what we should or shouldn't do.  In much of contemporary Christendom the concept of the separation of church and state is being pushed to mean the exclusion of God from human affairs, even though these concepts are not the same.

The experience of euthanasia in Nazi Germany earlier in this century left us with some eye-openers. It was endorsed, pioneered and implemented by medical practitioners of the highest order of intelligence and professional status.  Once the concept of "a life not worthy of living" was condoned and accepted, the foundation was laid for the kinds of decisions which eventually led to the horrors that followed.  Fifty years later, the euthanasia lobby has regrouped in the Netherlands and is targeting Europe and America. Their opponents question the alleged free consent of patients who, already in great personal distress, must additionally suffer from knowledge of the burden their illness and treatment is placing on their families, both psychologically and financially.  Furthermore, consent given by family is open to the possibility of conflict of interest.  The battle lines are drawn and the outcome remains to be seen, but this is a conflict that is avoided in Islam because of its firm theological strength.

## GENETIC ENGINEERING

Genetic engineering particularly has attracted lengthy discussions among Islamic scholars because of a phrase in the Quran about *"changing God's creation."*  According to the Quran, after Satan tempted Adam and Eve to sin by eating from the forbidden tree, he was dismayed to see them repenting and being forgiven and honored by their mission to populate Planet Earth as God's vicegerents. Satan then asked God to grant him another chance to prove that humans are not so trustworthy after all. When God granted the permission to tempt mankind (making it clear that he could tempt only those who opted to follow him), Satan disclosed some of his plots to confound them, saying: *"Verily of Thy servants I shall most certainly take my due share, and shall lead them astray and fill them with vain desires. And I shall command them so that they cut off the ears of cattle (in idolatrous sacrifice), and I shall command them and they will change God's creation"* (4:118-119). This verse has deeply influenced the verdicts of Islamic scholars and opinions of medical practitioners regarding related issues. For example, this verse has a bearing on the issue of sexual conversion operations, whereby men try to turn themselves into women and vice versa. While the verse clearly applies to such radical and unnatural surgery, the consensus is that this Quranic verse cannot be invoked as a total and radical ban on genetic engineering. If carried too far it would conflict with many forms of truly curative surgery that also entail some change in God's creation.

Many ethical issues are raised by the scientific development of genetic engineering. The creation of new virulent bacteria for use in biological warfare was a serious concern of the early seventies when the technology of recombinant DNA was first described. Such an application is clearly wrong. Applications such as the diagnosis, amelioration, cure or prevention of genetic disease are acceptable and even commendable. Gene replacement is essentially transplantation surgery, albeit at the molecular level. The pharmaceutical possibilities of genetic engineering may open tremendous vistas in the treatment of many illnesses, and the possibilities in agriculture and animal husbandry might help solve the problem of famine the world over.

The main concerns about genetic engineering lie in the area of the unknown and unsuspected future. The possibility of grafting new genes not only in somatic cells but also into germ cells, thus affecting coming generations, could later be associated with tragic self- perpetuating mutations. The hazards of atomic radiation were not apparent for some time, nor could the damage be repaired, and the stakes in genetic engineering are far more serious.

The introduction of genetic material from one species into another practically means the creation of a new species with mixed features. If pursued recklessly, with man's inclination for seeking the unknown until it is known and the unachievable until it becomes achievable, mankind may be confronted by patterns of life yet to appear on the biological stage. If this happens, scientists might think that everything is under control while the case is not really so. Manipulating human progeny might even be extended beyond combatting disease to the cultivation of physical characteristics considered desirable, leading to elitism and discrimination against (normal) individuals who lack those characteristics. Worse still would be the attempt to manipulate behavior by isolating the genes that shape it. An attempt to tamper with the human personality and its capacity for individual responsibility and accountability would certainly be condemned by Islam.

Genetic engineering technology itself attracts large capital for investment, and its investors will inevitably seek maximal financial return. Many scientists have already exchanged their ivory towers for golden ones and the spirit of open and altruistic cooperation for trade-secrecy and patenting forms of life. Moral concerns have been voiced that bear on equity, justice and the common good. Perhaps it is time for a comprehensive public debate and the prospective formulation of an ethical code for genetic engineering. A long story is in the waiting, and it is just beginning to unfold.

# Epilogue

It would be a pity if this book was simply read and then tossed aside like any other. Even if the discerning reader believes every word I have written and stops at that, I will have failed in my purpose. Unless the cognitive stage moves on to a psycho-motor stage, my mission will remain unaccomplished. If the knowledge presented in these pages generates no feeling (in the reader's heart) and is not reflected in behavior, it will remain sterile like a tree that bears no fruit.

Hearts cannot harbor a vacuum and must be filled with love, hate or indifference. In my late sixties, and after life-long study, reflection and insight into my Islamic faith, I feel my heart bursting with love. It is nonspecific love that has no address attached to it. I feel love towards my fellow humans, animals, birds, trees, things, the earth and the universe in which we live, and deep in my heart I wish it were contagious.

Love cannot be a replacement for politics, economics, industry, management, labor, business or even war. But people's actions are invariably propelled by their attitudes, their launching pads. So far these have predominantly been selfishness, greed, creed and insensitivity, which regrettably operate both at the individual and at the international level. If that could change, then all would be happy, even those who would sacrifice their lifestyle for the common good of all.

The philosophy of love as a basic motivation is not new, but in our times most people do not seriously embrace it. It extends across religion and race, hence the importance for its adherents to reach out and join one another. To be in the minority is no deterrent, if the curve of goodness keeps rising. It is a need felt by all of humanity. People are fed up with materialistic solutions and the deceit of atheism, and there is a spiritual thirst that yearns to be quenched. If a minimal critical mass of those who are willing to strive for goodness and decency in life would only take the initiative, they could generate a chain reaction with sweeping power. The world could change. But that will never come about without diligent, selfless effort on the part of those who believe in its importance.

I conclude with the Islamic greeting: Peace be upon you.

# Glossary

Allah.  The Arabic proper name of the One God, the Creator and Lord of the universe, the God of Adam, Noah, Abraham, Moses, Jesus, Muhammad, and all the prophets.

Allahu akbar.  God is greater than all else. Recited by Muslims in the *adhan*, in their prayers, and as supplication and praise of God at any time.

eid.  Feast or festival.  Muslims have two *eids*, the first celebrating the completion of the fast of *Ramadan*, the second commemorating Prophet Abraham's obedience to God.  Muslims celebrate these *eids* with special congregational prayers, acts of charity and gatherings with family and friends.

hadith.  The recorded statements of the prophet Muhammad, memorized and written down by his companions and later compiled in various collections.  Of these Bukhari and Muslim are the two most authentic. Other authentic collections are Muwatta, Al-Nisa'i, Ibn Majah, Al-Tirmidhi, and Abu Dawud. Sometimes referred to as "tradition," *hadith* is the second major source of Islamic law after the Quran. The science of *hadith* is scrupulous in ascertaining the authenticity of any *hadith* of the Prophet and the reliability of those reporting it.

hajj.  The pilgrimage, in the month of Dhul Hijjah, to the Kaaba, or the first House built for worship of God by Abraham and his son, Ishmael, in what is now known as the city of Makkah (Saudi Arabia). Hajj concludes with the Feast of Sacrifice (*Eid ul Adha)* and is mandatory for all Muslims who can afford the journey to Makkah physically and financially, at least once in life.

ijtihad.  Lit. "striving," in Islamic law it means putting forth maximum effort through juristic reasoning in regard to a problem or issue, to ascertain the injunction of Islam and its real intent, especially when no specific guidance in original sources (the Quran and sunnah) is available.

imam. The leader of a congregational prayer or the elected ruler of a community.

Injil. The book revealed by God to the prophet Jesus for the guidance of the Children of Israel. It is no longer extant in toto, but parts of the original may have survived in the Gospels.

Islam. Lit. "submission" or "surrender," Islam means obedience and submission to God. *Islam* also means "peace," underlining the fact that it is only through obedience to God that man can achieve real peace with himself and with other forms of God's creation around him. Those who believe and practice Islam are Muslims. The *Quran* teaches that all of God's prophets, since the creation of man, were in this sense Muslims, and that their core message to mankind was Islam or the message of peace and obedience to God.

jihad. Lit. struggle. Denotes the struggle in the cause of God, whether it is directed at betterment of one's morals, reformation of one's character, or struggle in a wider social circle to curb evil and help promote good, peacefully and through beautiful exhortation, but also by use of force when tyranny and injustice prevail, depriving man of human dignity, freedom of thought, belief, and expression.

Kaaba. Lit. a cube shaped building, the Kaaba was the first mosque, built by Prophet Abraham and his son Ishmael in Makkah, for the worship of God.

Quran. The last book revealed by God as a guidance and mercy to all mankind. The *Quran* confirms what remains of the authentic revelations of God, guides man to the worship of God, instructs humanity about His true nature and His will for humankind, and explains the reality and purpose of our life on earth. It was revealed to the prophet Muhammad through the angel Gabriel over a period of twenty-three years.

Ramadan. The ninth month of the Islamic calendar, during which healthy adult Muslims must fast from food, drink, and conjugal relations from dawn to dusk. *Ramadan* falls eleven days earlier each year, a blessing which ensures that Muslims in neither the Northern or Southern hemispheres will be permanently required to fast for longer or shorter hours.

salah. The formal five mandatory prayers in Islam, during which Muslims recite portions of the Quran, bow and prostrate in worship. *Salah* puts Muslims in continual communication with their Creator, while providing a constant reminder of their higher moral and spiritual mission in life.

sawm. Fasting. *Sawm* is obligatory for Muslims during the month of *Ramadan* and a recommended optional practice during the rest of the year. Fasting trains Muslims in obedience to God, patience in times of hardship and compassion for the poor. As a form of worship, *sawm* is an intensely spiritual experience that enables conscientious Muslims to deepen their relationship with God.

shahadah. The declaration of faith, or the statement that there is no god but the One True God and that Muhammad is His servant and messenger. The only prerequisite to becoming Muslim is to recite the *shahadah* with sincere conviction.

Shari'ah. The Islamic law, derived from the *Quran*, the *sunnah* of the prophet Muhammad, and juristic reasoning (*ijtihad*) in matters not specifically delineated in the other two sources.

shi'a. Lit. a partisan. Denotes the minority of Muslims who believe that Ali, the cousin and son-in-law of the Prophet, was his legitimate successor rather than Abu Bakr (the first caliph) or others. While agreeing with other Muslims in the basic principles of Islam, the *shi'a* have nonetheless retained their identity as a distinct religious group.

shura. Mutual consultation. Muslims are ordered by the Quran to make decisions through the process of *shura*, which involves the selection of leaders through public mandate and leaders' consulting with those they represent when making decisions that will affect them. Muslims governments are obliged to follow the methodology of *shura*. There is no place for dictatorship in Islam.

sunnah. Lit. "the practice" or "example," *sunnah* comprises the actions and statements of the prophet Muhammad, and is a major source of Islamic law.

wudu. Ablutions. For Muslims every *salah* is an audience with their Lord, and they prepare for that audience by renewing their physical and mental state of purity with *wudu*, washing their hands, arms, face, and feet with clean water, and wiping heads and necks with wet fingers, while intending worship and adoration of God.

zakah. Lit. purification and growth. *Zakah* is also mandatory for all Muslims possessing wealth beyond their legitimate essential needs. They must give away 2.5% of any remaining money over and above their own legitimate needs to the poor and the needy.

# Index